Finance for Small and Entrepreneurial Businesses

The financial environment of small and entrepreneurial firms is changing rapidly and is a topic where significant disagreement remains amongst researchers and policy advisers. This concise textbook provides a comprehensive overview of the current and projected trends in this market for the benefit of students of entrepreneurship at an advanced level.

Written by an expert on small and medium-sized enterprise (SME) finance, it provides a straightforward review of the external funding choices faced by small business owners, drawing on a range of new data sources which have emerged in recent years, along with a range of case studies. In addition, it includes an analysis of longer-term trends and the role of the changing phases of the business cycle to equip readers to better understand the wider market environment both now and in the future.

Roberts provides students of entrepreneurship with everything they need to know to excel in understanding the financial environment and its effect on small business.

Richard Roberts is Hon. Professor at Birmingham University Business School, UK. Prior to this, he researched small businesses issues at Barclays for 30 years. During this period, Professor Roberts was a member of the BIS/HMT Small Firms Advisory Panel and the BBA Business Finance Taskforce. As well as his current Professorship, Richard is consultant to a number of public and private bodies, including the Treasury Select Committee, and holds an MBE for services to UK Small and Medium-Sized Businesses.

Routledge-ISBE Masters in Entrepreneurship
Edited by Susan Marlow and Janine Swail

The **Routledge-ISBE Masters in Entrepreneurship** series offers postgraduate students specialist but accessible textbooks on a range of entrepreneurship topics. Collectively, these texts form a significant resource base for those studying entrepreneurship, whether as part of an entrepreneurship-related programme of study, or as a new, non-cognate area for students in disciplines such as science and engineering, helping them to gain an in-depth understanding of contemporary entrepreneurial concepts.

The volumes in this series are authored by leading specialists in their field, and although they are discrete texts in their treatment of individual topics, all are united by a common structure and pedagogical approach. Key features of each volume include:

- A critical approach to combining theory with practice, which educates its reader rather than solely teaching a set of skills
- Clear learning objectives for each chapter
- The use of figures, tables and boxes to highlight key ideas, concepts and skills
- An annotated bibliography, guiding students in their further reading
- Discussion questions for each chapter to aid learning and put key concepts into practice.

Entrepreneurship
A Global Perspective
Stephen Roper

Female Entrepreneurship
Maura McAdam

Resourcing the Start-Up Business
Creating Dynamic Entrepreneurial Learning Capabilities
Oswald Jones, Allan Macpherson and Dilani Jayawarna

Entrepreneurship, Small Business and Public Policy
Evolution and revolution
Robert J. Bennett

Finance for Small and Entrepreneurial Businesses
Richard Roberts

This book reflects the accumulated knowledge of someone who really knows about the nitty-gritty of small business finance from working for 30 years for Barclays Bank, whilst writing top quality academic papers and being a major influence on policy. Nobody knows more and I urge you to read it.

David Storey, Professor, School of Business Management and Economics, The University of Sussex, UK

A number of us have been waiting for this book for a long time. It provides a unique insight into SME finance. It is well written and makes an important contribution to the SME policy and research literature.

Robin Jarvis, Special Adviser to Association of Chartered Certified Accountants (ACCA) and Professor of Accounting, Brunel University, UK

Finance for Small and Entrepreneurial Businesses

Richard Roberts

LONDON AND NEW YORK

First published 2015
by Routledge
2 Park Square, Milton Park, Abingdon, Oxon OX14 4RN

Simultaneously published in the USA and Canada
by Routledge
711 Third Avenue, New York, NY 10017

Routledge is an imprint of the Taylor & Francis Group, an informa business

British Library Cataloguing-in-Publication Data
A catalogue record for this book is available from the British Library

Library of Congress Cataloging-in-Publication Data

Roberts, Richard G.
Finance for small and entrepreneurial businesses / Richard Roberts.
pages cm. — (Routledge-ISBE masters in entrepreneurship)
Includes bibliographical references and index.
1. Small business—Finance. 2. New business enterprises—Finance. I. Title.
HG4027.7.R593 2015
658.15—dc23 2014036607

ISBN: 978-0-415-72099-1 (hbk)
ISBN: 978-0-415-72100-4 (pbk)
ISBN: 978-1-315-86664-2 (ebk)

Typeset in Perpetua and Bell Gothic
by Apex CoVantage, LLC

Printed and bound in Great Britain by
TJ International Ltd, Padstow, Cornwall

Dedicated to the memory of Mike Young, Southampton City Football Club supporter and Bank of England Official

1951–2012

Contents

Figures

Tables

Preface

The idea for this book came from a conversation with Professor Sue Marlow, one of the Editors of this series of books, while we were chatting on the fringe of an ISBE conference a couple of years ago. Knowing I was thinking of retiring from my job at Barclays, she suggested I needed to write something down. (Presumably she was worried I may forget everything!) I thank both the Editors for the invitation and hope the book meets their requirements.

My objective all the way through this book has been to write something which is not a standard textbook on finance, nor a practical guide on how to raise finance. I wanted to produce something that combined the practical experience of researching small business finance for 30 years or more with the additional observations made from within a large clearing bank. I hope I have managed to do both.

I would like to say thank you to everybody who has helped me in a professional capacity in my years at Barclays, both inside the bank and in the wider world of small and medium-sized enterprise (SME) research. All have made a contribution to this book. Indeed, the small business research community has a core informal membership of people at government departments, advisory committees, professional bodies and representative groups as well as the academic community. As a result, while some may have moved employers at times, I seem to have been working with the same people for a long time. Obviously, any good ideas in this book have come from numerous discussions over the years with this community.

I would still like to highlight a few people to thank more directly. First, my ex colleagues at the Barclays SME Research Team (especially Julian Frankish, David Miles, Gail Behan, Richard Froud and Rupert Anderton). As well as researching together, they had to put up with me as a Research Director day-to-day. Second, Professor David Storey, who I first met on the ESRC Small Firms Initiative in 1990, part funded by Barclays. He persuaded the bank to develop an in-house research capability and acted as informal adviser, mentor and co-researcher to the team for most of the next 15 years or more.

I have dedicated this book to my old friend Mike Young. Many will remember his years of work at the Bank of England in the area of small business finance.

He is greatly missed and my one regret is that I have written this book without the chance to have his direct input to its contents. He has no doubt still made numerous indirect contributions based on discussions back to the 1980s.

Julian Frankish from the Research Team and Toby Billington, another ex-Barclays colleague, have both helped me enormously reading through the draft and putting me right on a number of aspects of style and the odd legal point. I remain wholly responsible for any remaining errors and omissions.

Finally, of course, I add my thanks to the family, especially Anne, who have put up with me learning to produce a book again after 30 years of writing short business style reports.

Richard Roberts
July 2014

NOTE ON SOURCES, BIBLIOGRAPHY AND DATA

A selected bibliography is included at the end of each chapter. In addition, where appropriate, a data sources section is included in some chapters.

Part I

Context

Chapter 1

Defining small and entrepreneurial business finance

Small business finance differs in a number of ways from corporate funding, as do the external products available to both types of firm. In this chapter, two different but linked definitions are addressed:

1. The dual role of finance in business activity; finance provides a day-to-day input to production in addition to funding new capacity.
2. How the requirements of small and entrepreneurial firms differ from larger enterprises and corporate finance.

Both of these issues are key to the review of products to provide external finance for small and entrepreneurial firms that follows in subsequent chapters.

THE ROLE OF FINANCE IN BUSINESS ACTIVITY

Finance has a dual role in business life. First, it can be regarded as an element of the means of production as it enables the business to purchase raw materials and labour as well as service and maintain equipment and premises. In this context, any shortfall in the availability of funding can disrupt day-to-day business activity. A shortfall typically occurs when a mismatch is evident between the flow of income from sales against the required pattern of bill settlement or payment of wages. The day-to-day management of cash-flow is a balancing act undertaken by all business owners. For some firms, this is more difficult than others leading to the popular – and probably correct – assertion that more firms cease to trade because they run out of cash rather than become truly unprofitable.

Second, finance in business is needed to purchase capital plant to provide the core of the productive capacity of a firm. This capital plant can be in the form of property, equipment or vehicles. For many people, this core funding is regarded as the permanent capital of a firm. (It can be contrasted with all types of debt held by a firm that eventually need to be repaid in full.) However, in reality, this is only part of the story. Some of the core capital of the business may be needed to fund operations day-to-day until orders are won and production starts. It is not permanent in the sense of being fixed and unusable. The capital is used until the venture is successful enough to fund itself. This is pre-revenue funding to rent premises, pay staff and start marketing. The amount of pre-revenue funding needed and its duration will vary from business to business. Some of this variation is determined by industry sector. However, in part, pre-revenue can reflect the choices made by the business founders, particularly the commitment and effort they are willing to put into the launch of the venture to get it going. In addition, the funding need is also influenced by the ability of the start-up team, notably in such things as networking skills and the contacts they have to get a venture up and running.

Initially when the business is first set up the capital outlay should be comparatively high as the productive capacity is built up and pre-revenue activities are commonplace. A similar peak in use of finance for this purpose should be evident in any subsequent period of expansion. Moreover, finance of this type is more closely associated with the risk involved in any new venture or project. Typically, this finance should be regarded as more entrepreneurial than the day-to-day purchase of labour and materials to complete agreed orders. In most businesses using entrepreneurial finance this way the owners and investors of the business are likely to have much more at risk than from day-to-day trading. If the venture fails, assets may be sold and in many cases the founder investors will have to use core capital to fund a loss (perhaps a 100% loss and the closure of the business). However, if the venture succeeds, the investors will be the beneficiaries from its future profits.

The dual role of finance is summarised in Figure 1.1. Finance is needed in the day-to-day activity of a business to ensure a smooth production process. Cash-flow management is essentially a balancing act between incoming revenue from sales and payments out for the variable components of production. This is the basic financing need for all small firms (and the only one for many of them once a business has been established).

However, at various points in a business lifespan, firms have an additional funding requirement to create, replace and expand the productive capacity of the venture and fund pre-revenue activities; this is entrepreneurial finance. All new firms need this type of funding to a degree at start-up. After a business has been established, this additional and ongoing funding requirement is particularly evident in the minority of firms that survive, expand and create employment.

The distinction between cash-flow and productive capacity may appear at first glance to be too stylised to be used in business analysis. However, the contrary is actually the case. Many business owners ignore or confuse the distinction, often to the peril of the success of a venture. Simply categorising a business between its needs for cash-flow as opposed to capacity finance is itself a useful tool. Table 1.1 provides an illustration on how the definitions for cash-flow and entrepreneurial finance can be applied across a range of business types.

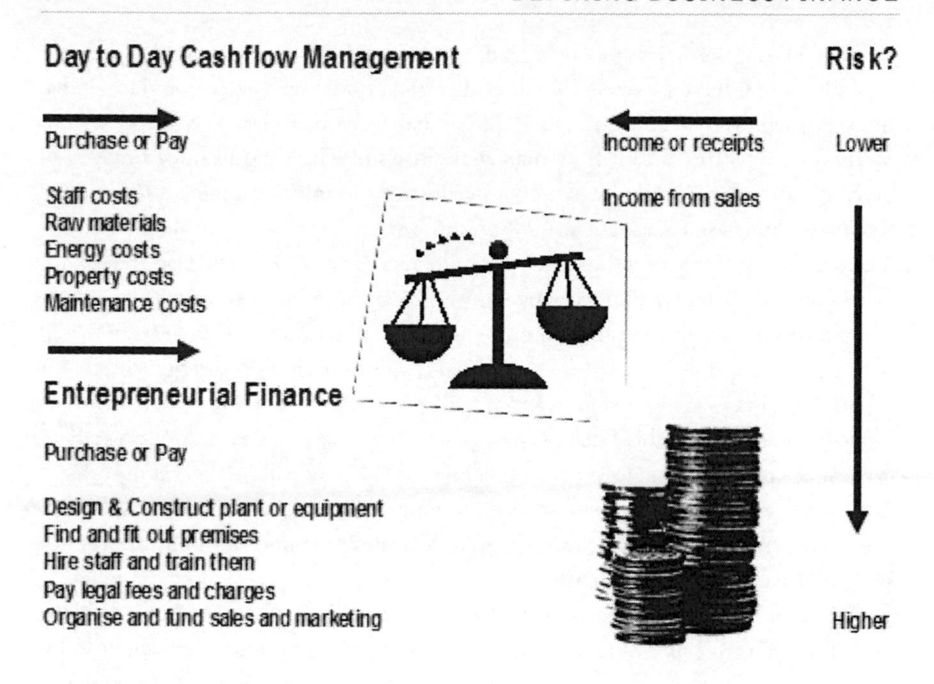

Figure 1.1
Day-to-day cash-flow management

Table 1.1 *Business Types and Funding Needs*

	Business Type	*Finance Type*
Farmer	Third generation family firm	Cash-flow
Builder (1)	Small jobbing builder	Cash-flow
Builder (2)	Speculative house builder	Entrepreneurial
Retail (1)	Corner shop	Cash-flow
Retail (2)	New online venture	Entrepreneurial
Manufacturer	Established firm, new overseas plant	Both
IT Services (1)	Laptop repair shop	Cash-flow
IT Services (2)	Games design and licensing	Entrepreneurial

A shop retailer, for example, may not have to wait too long to get paid as these are normally daily takings over the counter. However, as these sales receipts accumulate in the firm's bank account, a cash-flow requirement still exists to pay salaries and suppliers. The terms of trade agreed by the shop owner with a supplier could require bills to be settled 60 days after the goods were delivered. Hopefully, the stock will have been sold before the bill has to be paid; however, this may not be the case, creating a cash-flow management issue. The shop premises may well be rented from the freehold owner, so reducing the initial capital outlay needed to open a business to a lease premium and a month's rent in advance; but, any monthly or quarterly rental payments would also need to be settled on time.

In contrast, a new manufacturing firm is much more likely to have to purchase or build from scratch specialist equipment and production facilities even before it is in a position to bid for orders. As a result, the initial funding requirement for capacity purposes will be significant as will pre-revenue funding. Once an order book has been filled, this business will also order materials and employ staff to commence production. However, the delivery time may still be several months or even years away; in such circumstances, the purchaser is likely to have agreed to stage payments when certain production milestones have been met but the vendor will still have to manage the cash-flow.

All business types can be reviewed and considered by reference to the likely need for different types of finance. In part, the balance of funding by type is influenced by sector. However, it is also linked to the current phase of the business lifespan (start-up, mature, growing and diversifying into new products). The categorisation can change for the same firm over time as the needs of the business develop. A successful start-up will move from an entrepreneurial funding stage to a cash-flow-based environment. An established larger firm may develop a new venture or expand. As a result, such a firm may need both types of funding at the same time with the two activities operating partly at least at an arm's length from one another.

The distinction between two different types of funding in business activity holds true in most cases. In specific circumstances the distinction is less evident. In particular, care needs to be exercised around the categorisation of certain types of activity that involve a degree of speculation. Similar issues can be seen in the categorisation of funding needs for many project-based activities. In effect, funding itself is the dominant raw material that combines together the entrepreneurial and cash-flow aspects of business funding.

As an example, if a property developer acquires a block of run-down vacant retail units, the expectation is that, once refurbished, the capital value of the site will rise as will rental income. This funding arrangement is predominately entrepreneurial. It is not the same as, for example, an arable farmer planting seed in the autumn in the expectation of a crop being ready to sell in the spring next year; the farmer's funding need is primarily cash-flow management-based.

Indeed, it can also be argued that nearly every start-up firm goes through a phase where the purpose of funding is less clear cut. This is in their pre-revenue business planning stage and is often associated with a scramble to get the venture off the ground. The term 'bootstrap funding' is used sometimes to describe this activity where an entrepreneur will look to any available source of cash to support development work, rather than look for external equity or a term loan. However, subsequent analysis in the chapters that follow will show that bootstrapping is more to do with a scramble to get any source of funding rather than confusion as to why the cash is needed in the first place. In all cases, pre-start firms are looking for entrepreneurial funding.

SMALL AND ENTREPRENEURIAL FIRMS VERSUS CORPORATE FINANCE

In very general terms, the distinction between cash-flow and entrepreneurial finance apply to all types of business. However, it is worth considering in more detail the distinction between small and entrepreneurial firms versus the wider topic of corporate finance.

Even a very brief survey of the literature on funding for business reveals an extremely wide range of definitions being used for microenterprise, small firms, small and medium-sized enterprises (SMEs), entrepreneurial funding, corporate finance and so on. In many cases, the definitions can be tied back to categorisation based primarily on the number of employees. In the UK, these size class definitions are drawn from the relevant European Union (EU) guidance (summarised in Table 1.2). In the case of SMEs, for example, this definition is normally used if a business has fewer than 250 employees.

However, the strict use of an employee-based size categorisation alone is not sufficient to decide if a business is an SME. Indeed, the limitation of this method is recognised by a number of national authorities – including the European Commission – and many have introduced a more complex two-stage test (although it is not commonly used in the UK). The second stage assessment normally involves looking at the shareholding structure as well as the number of staff. For example, a large independent firm with a tightly controlled family-based shareholder structure and management team may have a lot in common with the funding opportunities of a firm with 10 employees that is run by a partnership team. In contrast,

Table 1.2 *EU Definition of SMEs – Test 1*

Test 1	*Employees (n.)*	*Turnover (Euro)*	*Balance Sheet (Euro)*
Medium	<250	<50m	<43m
Small	<50	<10m	<10m
Micro	<10	<2m	<2m

Source: http://ec.europa.eu/enterprise/policies/sme/files/sme_definition/sme_user_guide_en.pdf

a business with 20 staff run by professional managers could be a 49% owned but non-consolidated subsidiary of a Plc. As such, this small business may have access to sources of finance that most firms of a similar size would envy. For example, a potential funder may well transfer at least some of the lower credit risk status of the major shareholder to the small firm and make a finance offer (or a lower-priced deal) (Table 1.3).

This study looks at the products used in external funding for small and entrepreneurial firms. It does not seek to be a review of corporate finance as a whole. As a simple guide, the following definitions are used in respect of small and entrepreneurial businesses:

- Small firms are established enterprises that have no access to financial instruments or securities for any form of debt and equity. Owners often have a high degree of overlap between business and personal assets; any savings or investments they hold are typically undiversified. The money tied up in the business venture represents most if not all of the owners' wealth, or debts are secured against the bulk of any non-business assets they own. Even if the business has a corporate structure, limited liability is compromised and not absolute (so owners have substantial personal value at risk from business failure). Normally small firms will meet the revised EU definition of an SME and have less than 250 staff. The majority of firms will be well below this size threshold.
- Entrepreneurial firms are typically small firms in a period of change or transition. This can be a business start-up or a growth phase; in some cases it could also be a firm looking at funding a business turnaround.
- A large firm is a business that has either direct or indirect access to a range of capital markets to fund loans and equity. Moreover, the ultimate owners of the business do have effective limited liability and diversified investment portfolios. The firm will probably have a number of lines of commercial activity in operation concurrently. Some of these may exhibit entrepreneurial

Table 1.3 *EU Definition of SMEs – Test 2*

Test 2	*Shareholding Structure**	*Accounting Structure+*	*EU Definition*
Autonomous	<25%	Simple	Small
Partnership	25% to 50%	Simple	Medium
Linked	>50%	Consolidated	Large

Source: www.ec.europa.eu/enterprise/policies/sme/files/sme_definition/sme_user_guide_en.pdf

* Does not own more than this percentage of another business or this level of share is not owned by another firm

+ Is the accounting structure of the enterprise simple (unconsolidated) or consolidated as part of a larger group?

characteristics of growth or change but these will not compromise the funding environment for the whole entity. The analysis of the financing needs and characteristics of large firms is interchangeable with the study of corporate finance. Normally, large firms will fall outside the revised EU definition of an SME and have more than 250 staff. While collectively very important for overall economic activity and employment, these firms are few in number. Large firms and the external funding products they use are excluded from this review (unless they are used by both large and small firms).

OVERALL APPROACH AND OUTLINE OF CHAPTERS

The following chapters of this book, first, identify and, second, contain an analysis of the external funding products for small firms and entrepreneurial firms. The separate chapters on each product include a review of:

- The product scope and its use either for day-to-day or entrepreneurial purposes.
- The main suppliers.

This is followed by a discussion on funding choices over the duration of both a business lifespan and through changing economic circumstances (including a review of the role of public policy).

BIBLIOGRAPHY

HUGHES, A. Finance for SMEs: a UK perspective, *Small Business Economics*, 9 (2), pp. 151–166, 1997.

HUGHES, A. and STOREY, D.J. (eds.) *Finance and the Small Firm*, London, Routledge, 1994.

STOREY, D.J. and GREENE, F. *Small Business and Entrepreneurship*, London, Financial Times Press, 2010.

Chapter 2

Why is lending to – or investing in – a small firm difficult?

Lending money to anyone or buying any form of financial investment involves a degree of risk. Providing a loan facility to a sovereign government or a blue-chip company has some risk of default. Even so, billions are lent by banks to these borrowers every year. Also, thousands of retail investors buy shares in companies every day and an even greater number do so indirectly as well via unit trusts and pension funds.

However, without exception, direct commercial lending or investing in small businesses is commonly regarded as a specialised activity with some unique characteristics and risks. While later chapters review current attempts to introduce a new group of smaller lenders and investors into the small business funding market place, the perception that this is a specialised finance market persists.

A common misconception is that the difficulty in dealing with small business finance markets is the level of risk itself. Small businesses do have a much higher risk of default than blue-chip firms. For example, across the whole small business market place in the UK, even in a good year for trading, over 10% of all firms will cease to trade and around 2.5% of firms with a loan will default on payments. This default rate is at least five times greater than amongst listed companies. Although the likelihood of default for listed companies is very low, the value of every default can be exceptionally high but this still does not appear to be a major barrier to finding lenders.

Even so, lending or investing requires acceptance of a degree of risk in order to obtain a financial return. Adjusting the price charged to accommodate for the degree of risk allows any financial service provider or external investor to accept a level of risk. In the case of a debt provider, the price will be reflected via the interest rate; for an equity investor, it will be reflected in the price paid to acquire the shares in the business and the anticipated share of any future profit. Of course, extreme cases of high risk can be seen as too difficult to support 'at any price'. However, these cases are rare. Many high street banks will already provide unsecured loan products to smaller firms with an assumed default rate of over 20%, although the interest rate could be close to 20% a year. Venture capital investors will probably achieve a portfolio return based on the profits from two investments in every five; the other three (i.e. 60%) would be a total loss. Consequently, a hierachy of products exist with different risk-reward (see Figure 2.1).

Rather than the degree of risk itself in dealing with smaller-business finance markets, many investors are put off by the uncertainty around the likely return. In effect, investors find it difficult to strike the correct price commensurate with the risk. Also, unlike other forms of financial investment, market liquidity is low, especially for equity investors, suggesting even if a mistake is made over an investment choice you may still be tied into a firm for some time. As a result, it is uncertainty of return rather than the level of risk itself that ensures small business external funding remains a specialist field of activity.

What are the particular issues in small business finance markets that lead to this heightened uncertainty? Three issues are cited by most commentators. Small business data is of mixed quality; it is often called an opaque market. As a result, the related issues of adverse selection and moral hazard are often cited as being very prevalent in this market. These are three core issues that attract a lot of academic research, which is not repeated here. Rather, a short outline of all three issues and what potential lenders and investors can do to address them provides a good starting point to look at individual financing products in more detail.

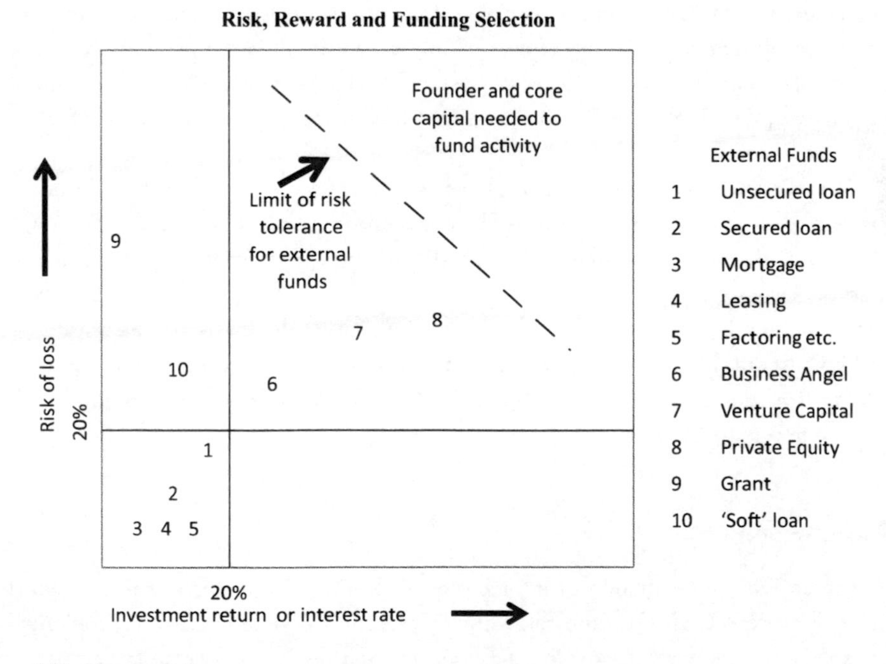

Figure 2.1
Risk, Reward and Funding Selection

OPACITY IN SMALL BUSINESS INFORMATION

The market information generally available about small firms is normally very limited in both scale and accuracy. Small businesses are normally privately owned. Most firms are owned by one person. For the minority that have multiple shareholders, these are often members of the same family.

The business owners may ultimately need to file tax-related information with the public authorities and in some cases a business register (such as Companies House in the UK). However, the depth and scale of the financial information is often very limited and only filed in arrears. This is in direct contrast with larger firms with publicly traded equity that have more detailed filing requirements and a specialised industry (brokers) looking at emerging business events, as well as professional investors and the financial press.

Of course, business owners should know everything about the underlying position of the business. However, because external providers are often much less well informed the balance of knowledge is one-sided. This asymmetric information is a market failure. In publicly traded equities and debt instruments, a legal sanction is in place to stop insider trading by the officials who hold this knowledge. However, these rules do not exist in unquoted company transactions for debt or equity (apart from general protection against fraud).

To overcome this problem, the credit reference industry has tried to collect and analyse what information is available. In some cases, firms being scrutinised volunteer information as well. However, this does not solve the problem. While credit information is valuable it is still essentially backward-looking. Also, while volunteered data is also useful, the control of its release is still in the hands of the business owner.

The existence of opaque or 'fuzzy' business information on smaller firms is not just a market failure in the provision of business information. Rather, as a knock-on effect, it is also a market failure in the small and entrepreneurial business finance market. The opacity, or lack of clarity, created by less than perfect information accessible to all generates the opportunity for incorrect decisions around lending and investment decisions. This is illustrated by the two related additional problems arising from information asymmetry that all external finance providers need to address in one form or another.

Adverse selection

The underlying poor quality of information makes it difficult for a lender or an investor to select who to fund rather than reject. Of course, the same problem does exist for the very largest firms as well but the level of uncertainty is much lower because the quality of information is much higher. The possibility of adverse selection refers to such an outcome. Either a 'good' applicant is denied funds or a 'bad' one is wrongly accepted. These two possible outcomes are often referred to as Type 1 or Type 2 errors, mirroring the outcomes of statistical hypothesis testing.

In a start-up situation, it can be argued that the roles are reversed. A funder may have more realistic and wider market knowledge than an entrepreneur. This could be used to leverage a deal on too favourable terms to them. In practical terms, reverse information asymmetry such as this is more likely to assist the funder in more correctly assessing who to decline and could indicate the market failure is less evident in some circumstances.

Moral hazard

In discussions between a finance provider and a business owner, questions will be asked in order to help assess risk. It is possible that the owner will control the flow of this information in order to help a favourable outcome. In order to obtain funding, an owner may accept an offer of a very high interest charge or projected dividend schedule that they know is unrealistic to fulfil. In many countries such activity may be illegal but even if not it raises a question about honesty.

However, the concept of moral hazard is much wider than a concern about honesty before a deal is arranged. Rather, the hazard extends to the behaviour of the business owner post the funding deal being arranged. Will the owner spend the funding in line with the business plan, or work as hard as promised to achieve the goal? Such issues form the core of many disputes between business owners and both debt and equity funders. Again, the heart of the problem is lack of information so moral hazard can also be called asymmetric information 'after the event' (while adverse selection is 'before the event').

ADDRESSING INFORMATION ASYMMETRY

All commercially based debt or equity investors will seek to reduce the incidence of adverse selection and moral hazard through a number of techniques. These activities fall into the following four main groups.

Assessing applicant quality

In debt markets, applications are normally appraised by a lender against a list of criteria; this may be a formal scorecard or, for larger loans, a series of tests applied against the business plan and other data supplied by the applicant. In the case of equity investors, going through a due diligence process before investment takes place is the norm. To varying degrees, a quality assessment will be included with all types of commercial finance products, as well as cash-flow-based activities.

Terms and conditions

Commercial funding is determined through assessment and negotiation. As a result, it is normal practice for an offer to supply finance to come with a range of terms and conditions as part of the deal offered back to the applicant. This may include regular access to private management information. A debt provider for both entrepreneurial and cash-flow purposes may include terms such as the receipt of regular loan repayments by a fixed date each month or the operation of banking facilities (not going over an overdraft limit). For an equity investor in an entrepreneurial venture, they may ask for a seat on the board of a company.

Asking for security and a personal stake

Debt and equity providers will often be reassured if the business owners have personal financial exposure to the risk of the newly funded activity. Security can also include charges over personal assets attached to the business debt obligation by way of a personal guarantee outside of any limited liability. Although most equity investors cannot have security as such, many of them will often structure a deal to include both debt and equity. (Some more complex equity arrangements do offer limited security options as well.) Providers of entrepreneurial funding will often ensure the owner has a personal stake ('skin in the game').

The price charged

Debt funding on commercial terms for entrepreneurial and most cash-flow activities has to be priced above the cost of funding to the financial institution (where the cost includes the administrative charge to assess the loan as well). How much over this cost will reflect the view of the funder of the risk involved in each case. As debt investors can only get the return of the original funds lent plus interest, they have to charge all borrowers an insurance premium to cover the likelihood that some of them will default.

How far debt interest can be used to exert influence over both adverse selection and moral hazard is a matter for some debate. If good borrowers are charged too much they may decide to use alternative funding, especially when a wide range of providers are active in the market offering a lower price. Only higher-risk applicants will pay the higher price as they have more limited choice. Hence, in an effort to control moral hazard, a debt investor can end up with more risky customers only.

An equity investor on the other hand can structure the price of an offer in a number of ways. The price they are prepared to pay for the shares is important. This can be in terms of a price per share or what percentage of the voting rights in a business they acquire for a fixed investment sum. However, investors can also make additional arrangements linked to the price such as an understanding with the Board on dividend policy or direct board membership. Consequently, equity investors will typically look to fund higher-risk ventures than debt providers. The greater insight and control over the business they have allows equity investors to accept a higher risk in exchange for the prospect of a higher financial return (as they have a right to a defined share of any future profits, unlike a debt investor whose receipt of interest is not linked to the success of the business). A key part in taking the higher risk is the enhanced assurances on the likelihood of a return through access to information from inside the management team.

CONCLUSION

Uncertainty of return rather than the absolute level of risk is the main reason why lending and investing in the small business market is seen as a specialised financial activity. This is particularly the case amongst entrepreneurial rather than established small firms. All funding – debt, equity or asset-based – seeks to reduce uncertainty through the appraisal of finance applications. This may be done simply via a standard scorecard or through a much less transparent interview and discussion process.

Moreover, a constant theme in this study is also to consider the techniques deployed by funders to try to control and reduce uncertainty. More examples of the activities commonly used are discussed in later chapters covering each of the product areas. Through looking at what funders want to achieve to control or at least better understand these risks on a case-by-case basis, applicants should find access to appropriate finance is easier to achieve.

BIBLIOGRAPHY

GIFFORD, S. Risk and Uncertainty. In ACS, Z.J. and AUDRETSCH D.B. (eds.) *Handbook of Entrepreneurship Research*, 2nd Ed., New York, Springer, 2011.

GREAT BRITAIN, DEPARTMENT FOR BUSINESS, INNOVATION AND SKILLS *SME Access to External Finance (BIS Economics paper 16)*, London, BIS (URN 12/539), 2012.

HUGHES, A. and STOREY, D.J. (eds.) *Finance and the Small Firm*, London, Routledge, 1994.

PARKER, S.C. *The Economics of Entrepreneurship*, Cambridge, Cambridge University Press, 2009.

STIGLITZ, J.E. and WEISS, A.M. Credit rationing in markets with incomplete information, *American Economic Review*, 71, pp. 393–410, 1981.

STIGLITZ, J.E. and WEISS, A. Credit Rationing and Collateral. In EDWARDS, J., FRANKS, J., MAYER, C. and SCHAEFER, S. (eds.) *Recent Developments in Corporate Finance*, Cambridge, Cambridge University Press, 1986.

Chapter 3

External finance products used by small and entrepreneurial businesses

Small and entrepreneurial businesses use a limited group of financial products in order to meet their external finance requirements. In this chapter, using data from the UK, the products for both the day-to-day and the capacity-building finance needs of small firms are identified. First, this is done by looking at the aggregate profile of financing of small firms in the UK. Second, the sources of external finance selected from the UK analysis are reviewed against similar data for key international markets.

EXTERNAL VERSUS INTERNAL FUNDING

Prior to looking at the external financial products used by small firms, it is also necessary to consider in more detail the circumstances in which they are needed. It could be argued that it would make sense if businesses never needed to use external finance at all either for cash-flow or expansion purposes; indeed, for many firms, this is their goal and operating practice and in such circumstances the use of any form of external finance reduces the immediate financial returns to the business owners to some degree. Many business owners look to achieve this position as well as it provides the firm with a degree of independence and security.

A large number of firms, as illustrated later in this chapter, report they do not use any external funding. These firms are fully funded from internal sources, mainly for cash-flow purposes without any plans for expansion or growth. While external commentators may well argue that the desire for financial independence may only be achieved at the expense of a firm reaching its full potential, it is very understandable, given the wide range of motivations people have for going into business in the first place, why the objective of self-sufficiency in cash-flow funding is attractive to many. However, this, in turn, creates differing views on the desirability of external finance when needed. For example, if a business owner needs to seek external finance products to address a cash-flow management problem, this is often seen by them as a necessary evil; they would rather not have the product but need it and have to accept the immediate associated reduction in business income. However, because the product has to be used grudgingly to offset a business problem, this often forms the origin of tension between the user and supplier of the product or service (perhaps about the quality of service or, in particular, the rate of interest on an overdraft facility).

In contrast, firms that are unable to fund in full an entrepreneurial phase in business development from internal sources more eagerly seek external suppliers to fill this gap. Indeed, given that entrepreneurial activity by definition is more risky than work to fulfil agreed orders on a day-to-day basis, it makes more sense for business owners to share the risk where they can. The 'pecking order' theory of funding is the term used to illustrate this phenomenon where business owners in such circumstances will seek other sources of funding to help share risk. However, the 'pecking order' process also means that external entrepreneurial funding is more welcome with owners willing to allocate a share of any expected increase in business revenues with someone else.

In practical terms, this means that firms using external finance for equipment and property purchase or business expansion are much more comfortable with using the associated products and paying the related costs than is the case for cash-flow products. Selling a part of the business through an equity stake is still a big step for any owner but generally most that do also report this to be a positive step towards a business goal. This provides a stark contrast with a discussion between a business owner and the bank manager about the cost of an overdraft facility the business needs to keep on a monthly basis to ensure security of cash-flow management, even though it is rarely used.

WHICH PRODUCTS?

While the issues discussed in both Chapters 1 and 2 apply to businesses in any geographical market, the UK has been selected as the basis for the identification of a range of financial products that will be reviewed in depth in subsequent chapters. Selecting a specific market is important for a later discussion of many aspects of the wider business environment and its impact on funding decisions. Using the SME Finance Monitor, a comprehensive review of market conditions in the UK is available. Based on the full results for 2013, Table 3.1 contains data on the external products that were used by SMEs.

In 2013, about 41% of SMEs in the UK were using some form of external finance in order to operate the business. The remainder – and the majority of them – were self-sufficient, being able to operate through cash-flow management and using the financial reserves of the business (or the personal savings of the owners).

Table 3.1 *SME Finance Products in use, 2013*

Percentages of UK SMEs, 2013	*Used in 2013*	*Applied in 2013*	*Success rate*
Overdraft (incl. renewals)	18	6	88/90*
Credit card	18	4	88
Term Loan or Mortgage (incl. renewals)	8	3	56/65*
Leasing/HP	8	4	87
Loans/Equity from Directors	5	3	90
Loans/Equity from Family/Friends	5	3	84
Grants	2	1	59
Invoice Finance	1	1	75
Loans from other 3rd parties	1	1	72
Equity from other 3rd parties	<1		
Any External Source	41		
Personal Funds Injection	33		
• *Out of choice*	18		
• *Out of necessity*	15		

Source: BDRC, SME Finance Monitor: The Year in Review, Q4 2013, February 2014

* Two different success rates are quoted. The lower rate is a positive outcome which is the product applied for. The higher rate is a successful funding outcome (including being redirected to successfully apply for a more appropriate product).

Indeed, regardless of using external funding or not, in one in three firms the owners decided to put in additional funds from personal resources in order to top up financial reserves. The motives for doing this were mixed; some owners decided they had to do it as they may have believed external funding would be difficult to arrange (or whoever was supplying the external funding made the cash injection a condition of agreement). Otherwise, some owners may well have wanted to retain full control of the business (and any future profits).

Using an external finance product in 2013

Looking at firms using an external finance product in 2013, cash-flow-oriented funding such as overdrafts and credit cards were by far the most common. This is not surprising as all firms need to trade day-to-day (which also ensures trade credit as a financial management practice is widely used as well). While similar numbers of firms use a credit card and an overdraft, about 10% of smaller firms use both at the same time. The credit card is normally regarded as the most commonly used external finance product, largely because the incidence of use is higher (a firm may have two or three credit cards held by directors rather than a single overdraft). The validity of this ranking is a matter of debate as most card purchases are low value and an overdraft or a structured loan may well provide a greater share of total external funding in monetary terms.

In terms of incidence of use, it is often the low percentage of SMEs that have a term loan or commercial mortgage that surprises many commentators. Only 8% of small firms overall held this product in 2013. This again reinforces the point that most small firms are not seeking to grow or develop; rather, they just need to trade on a day-to-day basis. It is also the case that leasing and HP is just as commonly used by firms as structured debt finance and in many industry sectors the products are effective substitutes for each other.

The common thread through most of the other sources of funding – including grant funding that is not a commercial activity as such – is the very low incidence of use in the small business population. This is even the case for invoice finance. Also, in a small business population of up to 250 employees, using any truly third-party equity (funded through a business angel or private equity) is exceptionally rare (well under 45,000 firms in operation in 2013 had *ever* raised funding this way).

Applied in 2013 and average success rates

The use of a product such as a 15-year commercial mortgage does not automatically provide too much information about recent availability of external finance as this product may well have been obtained by a business many years ago. Table 3.1 also provides data of the number of firms in the UK SME market applying for each product in 2013 alone and the corresponding application success rate.

Looking just at 2013 applications still suggests that overdraft and credit cards are the most popular external sources of funding. Indeed, in 2013 at least, the overdraft was a more popular product than the credit card measured this way, although in reality these products have been on par with each other for a few years. Structured loan applications were less popular that those for leasing and HP. Also, other types of external funding were still much less common, although the less than strictly commercial funding sourced from existing directors or friends and family appear to have been more common than in previous years (a point discussed in Chapter 10).

In terms of success rates, it is of some surprise to many people that the vast majority of applications for external funding overall are successful, even for overdraft and loans. For an overdraft, 90% of applicants overall ended up with funding (nearly all with an overdraft); the equivalent figures for credit cards (88%) and loans (65%) were also high. Leasing, which is a fully secured rental rather than debt activity, was higher than for structured loans though; indeed, it was close to those of non-commercial director and family funding. Success rates for invoice discounting were slightly lower, probably reflecting counter-party credit ratings, as discussed in Chapter 6.

THE RANGE OF SMALL BUSINESS EXPERIENCE

All reviews of a single national market in one year will inevitably provide an 'average' view of overall activity. The variations around this average are often just as important as the overall picture. A number of possible characteristics can be reviewed to look at the scale of variation. In Table 3.2, the use of two different products groups – overdraft and loan – are illustrated with reference to industry group, along with the injection of personal funds to the business. This suggests, for example, the overdraft is more commonly used – as is debt funding overall – in agriculture. Structured funding, on the other hand, is more common in hotels due to freehold investment. Moreover, the higher incidence of debt funding also appears linked to the use of personal funds.

In the product-specific chapters that follow, further analysis is provided about the different types of business that typically tend to use certain types of external funding sources, including industry where appropriate. However, additional attention is particularly given to the variation in use by size of business where the range of variation is considerably more marked than is evident for either industry or region of business location. While the overall incidence of use may be modest at

Table 3.2 *SME debt products and personal capital injection use: industry analysis, 2013*

Percentages of UK SMEs, 2013	*Applied in 2013 (new or renew)*		*During 2013*
	Overdraft	*Structured Loan*	*Used Personal Funds*
Agriculture	12	8	38
Manufacturing	7	3	31
Construction	6	3	38
Wholesale and Retail	8	4	36
Hotels and Restaurants	10	7	41
Transport	8	3	40
Property and Business Services	4	3	40
Health, Social and Community Firms	6	2	37
Other Services	3	2	37

Source: BDRC, SME Finance Monitor: 2013Q4, pages 53 and 71

a national level across business of all sizes, in some of the larger employment categories, product use significantly increases. For example, while only 2% of SMEs overall used invoice finance in 2013, this increased to 19% of firms between 50 and 249 employees, making it a very important source of cash-flow funding for this group.

Moreover, each small business is different and circumstances cannot be accurately described just from using these standard analyses based on industry sector, size or business age. To illustrate this point, contrasting case studies have been included in Appendix I to look at how different types of business use external finance. These provide a further introduction to the more detailed chapters on specific types of product that follow.

INTERNATIONAL COMPARISONS

This study of external finance primarily uses data on the UK market. However, a short review of some other national markets suggests the broad types of product selected for more detailed analysis are just as relevant in an international context.

Attempts at a country-by-country comparison of SME statistics are always difficult. National definitions can vary. For example, it is commonplace in North America for the category of SMEs to include firms with up to 499 employees rather than 249 in the UK and the European Union (EU) as a whole. Even within the EU, some national authorities have domestic definitions of an SME that differ from the European Commission. Banking data often looks at loans under a certain value threshold, rather than loans issued to businesses within an SME size-band.

As any international survey moves beyond the EU, the availability of data collected in a consistent format declines. A decade-long project led by the World Bank did collect a unique firm-level dataset covering patterns of funding in SMEs across 48 countries (where SME was defined as under 500 employees). The survey period covered 1999–2000 and reported in 2004. The results have never been updated but they do provide a historical benchmark to confirm that the core external financial products serving UK smaller firms are also valid in a wider international context.

Profiled against the average of all the country data reported in Table 3.3, the UK made more use of retained profits and savings and used fewer external finance products than many others. However, the World Bank results also illustrate again the need to take account of national circumstances when looking at the use of external products. For example, several countries, notably France, Germany, the USA and Canada, have substantial state-backed development banks and government funding schemes that the World Bank reported as being part of the other sources of finance, not commercial bank finance. This suggests that across national boundaries the type of supplier and the terms and conditions of

Table 3.3 External Finance for SMEs – World Bank Business Environment Data, 2003–2004

	Retained	External Products & Services					
		Total	Bank	Leasing	Equity	Other	Trade Credit
UK	63.9	28.7	13.1	11.6	2.9	1.0	7.5
USA	52.9	40.5	21.5	3.2	6.1	9.7	6.6
France	69.1	23.5	6.8	5.8	4.3	6.7	7.4
Germany	45.7	53.4	16.8	23.1	0.7	12.6	0.9
Italy	22.3	71.9	49.7	6.9	1.7	13.7	5.8
Spain	60.0	35.8	23.0	0.7	8.0	4.1	4.2
Singapore	54.8	39.0	28.1	7.7	1.2	2.1	6.1
Canada	51.5	44.0	23.5	8.4	2.4	9.7	4.6
Poland	41.4	55.2	15.4	27.6	4.5	7.7	3.4
Sweden	56.6	37.3	19.7	8.3	1.2	8.0	6.2
Average*	49.8	50.2	20.9	13.6	3.4	7.3	5.0

Source: author's calculations based on results from the World Bank Business Environment Data, see www.go.worldbank.org/RV060VBJU0

See also BECK, T, DEMIRGUC-KUNT, A., and MAKSIMOVIC, V. Financing patterns around the world: Are small firms different?, *Journal of Financial Economics*, 89, p. 467–487.

* Note the Average data has been calculated using weights from the World Bank firm level data survey

funding will influence the external funding products used, an issue compounded further by tax and business legislation. Consequently, a UK-centric focus continues throughout the chapters that follow (some additional comments on international variations are provided in Appendix II).

CONCLUSION – PRODUCTS FOR DETAILED REVIEW

Looking at both finance in use and applications made in 2013 in the UK suggests five core product groups cover the external financing activities for small and entrepreneurial firms:

- Overdrafts and Credit Cards
- Structured Debt Products
- Leasing and Hire Purchase (HP)
- Invoice Finance
- Third-party Equity

The inclusion of equity may appear at odds with its low level of use in the small business market as a whole. However, in order to address entrepreneurial business funding more directly, while non-commercial sources of external funding such as grant or family and friends are strictly out of scope, this review includes a discussion of third-party external equity. Further analysis of the variation in product use within different industry and size groupings of UK businesses illustrate the same five groups remain valid. A brief review of some major international economies also points to the same conclusion.

The following five chapters of this book take one of these product groups in turn. Each chapter provides more detailed definitions on the products under review, which types of business tend to use them and why. In addition, the chapter looks at the suppliers of these different types of product and what factors they take into account when deciding if they can agree to funding requests. Subsequent chapters of the book then move from a detailed product-by-product analysis to a more integrated view of external finance for small firms over time looking at how businesses change the sources of external funding as they survive and grow.

BIBLIOGRAPHY

BDRC *SME Finance Monitor, Q4 2013 Report*, London, BDRC, 2014. Note that all source data in tables and charts are referenced against the pages and tables in this Q4 2013 report. For further information see the data source information for this chapter.

STEWART C. MYERS, The capital structure puzzle, *The Journal of Finance*, 39 (2), pp.574–592.

DATA SOURCES

Most of the data series from the SME Finance Monitor are available free of charge online from a dedicated portal: www.sme-finance-monitor.co.uk/ (accessed 10 July 2014).

A direct link to a download of the Q4 2013 report used as the basis for much of the commentary in Chapters 3 and 10 is available using: www.bdrc-continental.com/EasySiteWeb/GatewayLink.aspx?alId=7397 (accessed 10July 2014).

Full datasets are available from the ESRC Data Archive: www.data-archive.ac.uk/

The UK SME Finance Monitor catalogue reference is: www.discover.ukdataservice.ac.uk/catalogue/?sn=6888&type=Data%20catalogue (accessed 10 July 2014).

The World Bank Business Environment Survey data can be accessed in full at: www.go.worldbank.org/RV060VBJU0 (accessed 6 September 2014).

Part II

Product review

Chapter 4

Structured debt: term loans and commercial mortgages

Debt is the most common type of external funding used by a business over its lifetime. Indeed, the role of debt funding is probably underreported by business owners. The personal wealth used to fund the start-up of a firm could be regarded as an informal loan from an entrepreneur's overall household wealth to set up a venture in the first place. Few business owners will see this as debt, although future drawings from a business may well be used to replace the initial capital sourced this way. Family and friends may also lend money on non-commercial terms to set up a venture and these funds normally need to be repaid.

All forms of debt share a common feature in that access to this source of funding requires an acknowledgement that the capital sum has to be repaid at some time in the future plus interest. Any exceptions will be not fully commercial arrangements, such as a soft loan from a family member (although family-sourced loans can also be on a commercial basis). Debt can be used for either entrepreneurial or day-to-day funding purposes. The main types of debt are identified in Table 4.1 as well as some of the typical characteristics associated with each of them. Chapter 4 concentrates on term loans and commercial mortgages, the two main types of structured debt in the small business market place. Chapter 5 reviews overdraft and credit cards, the main sources of debt finance for cash-flow funding.

STRUCTURED DEBT PRODUCTS

Term loan

A loan of this type is a specific debt for a defined project or purpose and, as the name suggest, with a predetermined bullet repayment date or amortisation schedule for the principal capital sum. As a result, term loans are normally used for entrepreneurial activities by a firm, not day-to-day finance.

As used in the small business market place, term loans have a repayment schedule agreed before the funds are drawn out; hence it is a structured product.

Table 4.1 *Types of Debt*

Debt Product	*Use*	*Suppliers*	*Term (years)*	*Security (Y or N)**
Term Loan	Entrepreneurial	Banks, individuals, other firms, P2P lenders	1–10	Y & N
Commercial Mortgage	Entrepreneurial	Banks, building societies, other direct lenders	5–30	Y
Overdraft	Cash-flow	Banks via current account	<1	N
Credit Card	Cash-flow	Banks, other direct providers	<1	N

* In practical terms, security can also be provided through a director's guarantee – see text

Normally the structure is for a regular capital reduction with interest (often called an amortisation plan). However, other possible arrangements are indicated in Table 4.2. In most cases the length of the repayment period (the term) is matched to the progress or completion of the overall project and the lifetime economic value of the assets purchased or manufactured. Most loans of this type from a mainstream commercial source will typically be for three, five or occasionally 10 years.

Over the last decade, given the high initial fixed costs of setting up funding arrangements and monitoring, the use of a loan for under three years is now much less common and most lenders have a minimum size (£1,000 or even slightly higher). Similarly, the use of this product for a term of 10 years or more has fallen out of favour. This trend is mainly a consequence of the shortening of product lifecycles, especially with the impact of technology. Production machinery, vehicles, information technology (IT) assets and office equipment are likely to be regarded as having little residual value after three, five or 10 years depending on the type of equipment, even though the equipment may, in reality, be still serviceable and in full operation.

Loans can be on a secured or unsecured basis. A secured loan is one where the borrower has created a legal charge over an asset or item of value that can be sold in order to repay the debt if the business is unable to fund repayments from trading receipts. The secured assets could be property freeholds, cash, share certificates and a wide range of other less commonly used items (such as gold or jewellery).

In the case of a business with limited liability – either as a company or a limited partnership–the security may take the form of a floating charge. This is a charge over

Table 4.2 *Typical Term Loan Structures*

Term Loan Structure	*Feature*
Amortising	Regular repayments of capital and interest over the period of the loan
Low start capital repayment	Pre-agreed interest only repayments at start of loan but higher repayments
Low start capital holiday	Interest only repayments to start. Borrower has some flexibility to decide when to start repayments (at which point loan repayments recalculated to repay over original term)
Bullet repayment	Interest only payments for whole of the term with one final repayment of capital at the end

all, or a specific pool, of the businesses assets. The security offered is only tied to a specific debt when a non-repayment occurs (referred to as a crystallisation event). A floating charge is useful where an asset base is being added to all the time, allowing a firm to more easily provide security for a range of debts. A floating charge also allows the business to acquire and dispose of assets subject to the charge in the normal course of business prior to any crystallisation event occurring. As such, it provides flexibility for business owners.

For unincorporated firms, a floating charge cannot normally be used. In bankruptcy law, an owner of an unincorporated firm cannot distinguish between business and personal assets in the same way as a director of a limited company. As a result, for a lender the future quality and value of any floating charge is less certain. As a result, if required, a sole trader or unlimited partnership would need to pledge assets as security on a case-by-case basis. In some circumstances for larger loans, a specific directly pledged charge may be appropriate. However, providing a direct pledge at the start of a loan increases the borrowers' costs and may tie-up later funding options. To avoid this problem all business owners (directors, partners and sole traders) can also offer a personal guarantee to provide security. In some cases, a debt provider may ask for both. In either the case of directly pledged security or a guarantee, the value of any equity in a family home is normally the most contentious asset type (and for most borrowers specific rules are in place about taking legal advice if such security is likely to be used, especially if the house is shared with a partner).

The availability of security lowers the risk of the lending and should be reflected in the interest margin charged on the loan. In contrast, wholly unsecured lending has no such protection and will typically be more expensive. However, unsecured loans tend to be available for a shorter term than secured loans, reflecting this higher level of risk. They are also typically offered for smaller amounts.

In the UK, most small business loans with an initial value of up to £25,000 are unsecured. The Consumer Credit Act, 1974 (amended 2006) provides a more regulated environment for all credit agreements to individuals – including non-consumer loans to sole traders and partnerships of up to three people – making it a lot more straightforward for credit suppliers to just offer unsecured products (even to small companies). However, a personal guarantee may still be offered to cover the debts of the firm by any business owner.

Commercial mortgage

A commercial mortgage is a particular type of longer-term structured lending used in the purchase of real estate. Strictly speaking, as used in modern-day finance, a mortgage takes the form of a note recognising a charge over any deed or certificate of title for a property. This has the effect of stopping the sale of the property without the mortgage holders consent. Any new owner would also be responsible for the debt secured on the legal title. Moreover, if the agreed repayment schedule on the secured debt is not maintained, the mortgage note can be used by the lender to take control of the asset and, if needed, force the sale of the property to repay the debt.

A mortgage is different from a term loan with security where the borrower pledges to honour repayments and, if needed, they may choose to sell the assets to provide a means of repayment. Failure to repay would then allow the lender to seek court action to gain ownership of the pledged assets. In a mortgage, the lender already has proprietorial rights over the asset in event of payment default. The enhanced rights underpin the provision of long-term funds with 15-year-plus deals being the norm. Also, the enhanced rights lead to commercial mortgages being offered with lower interest rates than term loans.

In some cases, the purchase of the property alone will be sufficient to generate revenue to meet the loan repayments (for example, a buy-to-let mortgage for a landlord). Otherwise, a mortgage to fund the purchase of a commercial property such as an office or shop will allow the business to develop a revenue opportunity to meet repayments. From the point of view of the lender, the way the revenue is generated is of limited interest; most attention is on how reliable the income flow will be. As a result, a commercial mortgage application for a buy-to-let-landlord may well centre mainly on the expected credit status of any likely tenants, comparing the flow of rental income to the cost of the mortgage. Additionally, a new start-up is less likely to use a commercial mortgage to fund premises and renting may be more attractive.

In contrast, the owners of a well-established business with a track record of securing longer-term contracts may well think about a commercial mortgage to buy the freehold of the premises they work from to secure better control over costs; or, if they already own the freehold, the business proprietors may take on a mortgage to raise cash to fund a new venture at low interest rates. In all cases, the loan is fully secured at all times through the mortgage note attached to the property title.

A significant feature for this type of structured loan is the term that is nearly always over five years in duration and is typically 15, 20 and 25 years long. Normally, short duration mortgages – five or 10 years – are used for buy-to-let property investments and the landlord could have access to significant capital appreciation as well as rental income to fund repayments. A property may well be sold before the end of the term with the underlying capital appreciation repaying the debt on the mortgage.

In contrast, longer-term mortgages are more commonly used to fund the core strategic property assets of firms. In some cases, a mortgage will be used to raise cash for a business using a property already owned. The cash will be then used to fund another part of the business venture. In all cases, the longer term of 15, 20 or 25 years is helpful to ensure that the monthly repayments on the loan are manageable. This is also a recognition that firms are unlikely to benefit from any exceptional property inflation. Also, the property may be so specialised that resale options are limited and the existing owner is highly likely to want to continue with the loan for many years, perhaps even to term.

WHAT SORT OF FIRMS USE TERM LOANS AND COMMERCIAL MORTGAGES?

Firms that use structured loans are normally engaged in increasing or extending the core assets of a business (Table 4.3). Hence, these are funds for an entrepreneurial activity rather than for day-to-day funding. Debt finance for this

Table 4.3 *Users of Structured Term Debt in the UK, 2013*

		By Employment Size-band			
Percentages	*All SMEs*	*0*	*1–9*	*10–49*	*50–249*
Use	8	5	13	20	26
Applied	3	3	5	6	5
*Successful**	56	50	59	85	85

Source: SME Finance Monitor, Q42013 Report, tables pages 47, 69 and 133

* To boost sample sizes, these are 18 month rates ending Q3, 2013. The size-band data includes author's estimates.

purpose is most appropriate where some or all of a number of circumstances are evident:

- The risk of non-payment is low. A lender's maximum return is capped at the original sum plus interest. As a consequence, only entrepreneurial activities that are lower risk will be of interest. (Higher-risk activities are more suitable for equity funding where the investor can balance the possibility of non-payment with that of future revenue and dividends.)
- The time from initial spend to revenue is low. Structured loans are not appropriate for use in a pre-revenue situation for any period of time. It may be that the lender would offer a short capital repayment holiday but the emphasis will always be on ensuring a revenue stream is available to meet regular repayments. This is consistent with a low-risk activity.
- The project's risk-reward ratio is average. Even in situations where the project has a revenue stream, if the level of debt is too high, modest fluctuations or unexpected variations in business revenue could threaten repayment activity.

SUCCESS FACTORS IN STRUCTURED LOAN APPLICATIONS

As the number of credit suppliers increases with the growing role for non-high street banks and other providers in this market, it is increasingly difficult to talk of a single set of rules to help a firm secure structured debt funding. Also, in most major economies the majority of loan applications are already successful. Even so, data suggests the success rate varies quite noticeably with start-ups and those firms seeking a first loan much more likely to experience problems than older, established firms. In addition, the high overall average success rate hides a poorer outcome for firms seeking to grow rapidly with debt funding, or trying to introduce innovative products. As a result, it is important for entrepreneurial firms in particular to look at a funding proposal through the more critical eye of a potential supplier, rather than the rose-tinted view of an eager business founder keen to open a venture or expand (Figures 4.1 and 4.2).

All suppliers of finance have to address an interrelated set of problems when deciding to lend money. To a degree, this applies in all parts of the external finance market but especially so in small business debt and equity-based products:

- Small-firm markets are characterised by experiencing asymmetric information. Business information is less readily available to an external funder as it is in the direct control of the owner.
- The knowledge gap created by information shortages, in turn, leads to a dual problem of potential adverse selection of who to fund and an increasing likelihood of non-compliant behaviour (termed a moral hazard). In simple terms,

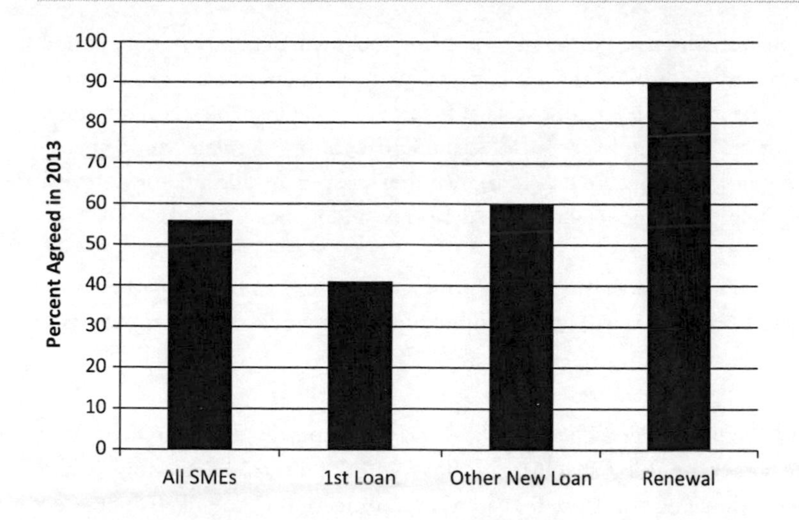

Figure 4.1
Term loan acceptance rate – by application type

Source: SME Finance Monitor Q4 2013, see Table 4.3

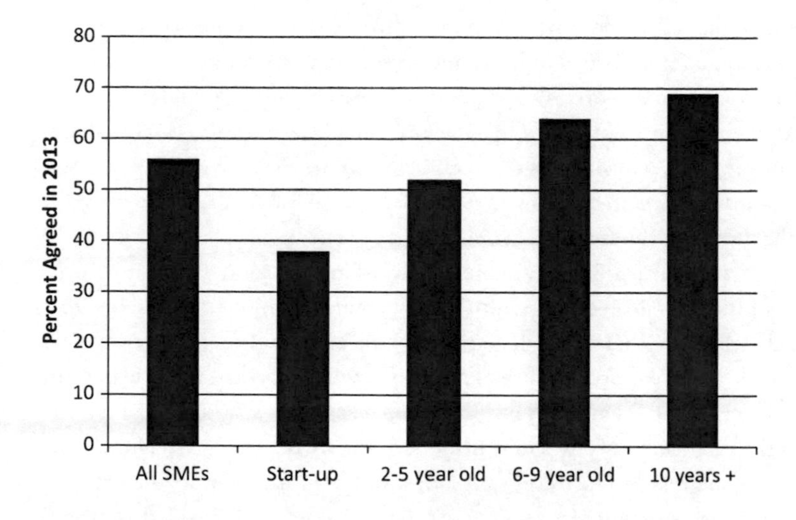

Figure 4.2
Term loan acceptance rate – by business age

Source: SME Finance Monitor Q4 2013, see Table 4.3

this is the possibility of too many business owners willing to take high commercial risk-seeking external funding, combined with an inability by funders to spot applications from this source correctly; as a result, low-risk applicants may have to pay a higher cost of funding to cover losses from reckless borrowers (or, in extreme cases, they could be denied funds).

The concepts were discussed in detail in Chapter 3 and will need to be kept in mind when looking at debt finance and are referred to again in later chapters on different types of finance. Suppliers of external finance to smaller firms – even though they may not refer to the issues of selection and hazard – implement screening activities that have the objective to minimise these issues. Applicants for external funding can help the supplier with these concerns and increase the likelihood of a successful outcome.

In general terms, for structured debt products, in order to meet supplier worries over selection and hazard, a few simple guidelines would appear appropriate in most circumstances:

- Identify for the lender a clear regular source of repayment for the debt. This can be shown by using surplus cash-flow you are already generating in the business. Alternatively, it can be based on a projection of the likely increased revenue obtained after using the loan to fund the investment. If projections are used, this is likely to be best presented in terms of a business plan that will be challenged by the supplier to see how robust it is. This scrutiny may go into significant detail for applications regarding large amounts of money.
- Remember that all lenders will be more impressed by a valid legal contract sitting behind a future projected revenue stream than a promise to work hard to find new customers (even though this promise is wholly genuine).
- Show the lender how committed you are to the project. In the case of structured loan finance, a business is often committing to repay over a long period of time. In these circumstances it is normal practice for small-firm owners to share the risk with the funder by having some of the owners' money involved in the venture. This is normally achieved by asking the lender to fund a proportion of the total project costs with the remainder coming from the owners' personal wealth – either through equity or a loan by the directors to the business – or the retained profits of the firm. Borrowing less than the full amount lowers the risk for the lender by reducing debt service costs. At the same time, sharing the risk illustrates the commitment of the owners to the scheme. (The lender will see this as illustrating the borrower also has 'skin in the game'.) How much risk-sharing – or leverage of bank funding – is needed is always difficult to judge but for smaller firms especially a 50:50 split is a good starting point.

While these guidelines will apply to all lenders, some suppliers have a more structured approach to lending decisions. This is particularly the case for the high street banks that still provide most of the loans in the market in the UK. Bank credit guidelines often use standard criteria to test applications and more specific guidance on this is included in Box 4.1.

BOX 4.1 HOW DOES A BANK DO IT?

The lack of perfect information in small-business credit markets obliges all debt providers to assess the risks involved in lending. All debt providers use a number of techniques to improve the quality of the decisions made. One of the most commonly discussed techniques is called the CAMPARI method of assessment. Most large retail banks have something like this approach, as do many other debt providers. This version is a slightly extended version called CAMPARI & SODA and applies in particular to applications for entrepreneurial debt finance.

C = Character	And	S = Stake
A = Ability		O = Organisation
M = Means		D = Demand
P = Purpose		A = Accuracy
A= Amount		
R = Repayment		
I = Insurance		

Most banks will use CAMPARI & SODA or something similar as a checklist to look at a lending proposition, although for smaller-value applications this may be implicit rather than explicit (for example, a relationship manager may just go through the checklist while thinking about the application). Also, the weight applied to each test will vary, although it is unlikely that any one of them would be ignored. We can consider each in turn.

Character

Are you known to the bank or can they easily check who you are? If you have a current account for a period of time and you approach the same bank for a loan they will already know a lot about you. Most banks will use behaviour scoring based on the way you operate your current account. If you go to another lender, they may well make background checks to confirm your identity and implement a credit check. For some in the credit profession the character check is seen mainly about a 'fit and proper person test' or a check of your willingness to pay your debts in the past.

Ability

What are your qualifications, experience or track record in relation to the loan being considered? This is especially relevant to entrepreneurial funding. Most banks will put a lot of emphasis on practical knowledge rather than paper qualifications.

Means

Do you have other funding to fall back on? As well as the money you have put into the venture directly, do you have access to other funds to help the business if needed? Banks do not want the first hiccup in a launch plan of a new venture to trigger a financial crisis. This data will also normally be judged as part of an ongoing banking relationship or a credit check.

Purpose

What do you want the money for? Is it legal? Also, does the business and financial planning look sensible? A bank will be worried by a proposal in which all the funding is drawn down as soon as it is sanctioned and used for a speculative activity. A preferred option would be for this phase of the entrepreneurial activity to be cash-funded with the bank's funds being drawn later as close to a revenue flow as possible.

Amount

Have the business owners got too little or too much money to complete the job? Do they need to spend as much as projected? Alternatively, have all the required sources of funding for an entrepreneurial venture been identified to ensure the project reaches fruition?

Repayment

Has the applicant identified a secure and large enough source of cash-flow to fund the scheduled repayments? If a long lead time is planned from inception to revenue, it is likely that the bank will suggest the stake by the business owners is higher. Or, if an existing business is seeking a round of entrepreneurial debt funding, does the existing business have enough surplus cash-flow to fund the repayments?

Insurance

If it all goes wrong, has the applicant got any security to offer? Would a personal guarantee help, especially if they have other personal assets?

Stake

How much has the borrower at risk in the venture? Most banks will start from a view that wholly new ventures should in most cases be 50:50 funded between debt and a personal stake. If the application has more than one person involved, do they all have some financial involvement in the enterprise?

Organisation

Is the business set up and operating on a sound legal footing? Does it have any outstanding legal issues to address that may impact on any financial reserves? Does it file its statutory information on time?

Demand

Especially where the bank operates a local relationship banking model, the customer's local manager will be able to pass comment on the application. High street managers will see many applications for the local market. While it would be inappropriate and in most cases illegal for a manager to tell a loan applicant that another entrepreneurial venture is in the pipeline locally that may impact on their business plan, a manager can use this information in the credit decision.

Accuracy

Do all the numbers add up? Especially if the loan applicant has not provided a formal business plan, the bank will check to see if the assumptions made around pricing and margins look sensible based on industry norms and local knowledge. Any significant omissions and errors would also be taken into consideration as part of the assessment of ability as well.

WHO ARE THE SUPPLIERS OF TERM DEBT FUNDING?

Suppliers of small-business term funding on commercial terms fall into three distinct groups across most national markets (Table 4.4).

Retail or high street banks

High street banks that supply money transmission facilities also supply term debt to customers. This activity developed out of their traditional cash-flow

Table 4.4 *Supply of Structured Term Loans in the UK, 2013*

£ billion	*Stock (year-end)*	*Origination (whole year)*
High Street Banks	92	21
Other Banks	61	22
Community Finance	0.5	0.15
P2P/Crowdfunding	0.3	0.193
B2B Corporate Loans	*	*
Public Sector	0.1	0.1
*Total**	160	45

* Includes an assumption for B2B corporate loans

Sources
(1) Bank of England, Bankstats, Table A8.1, May 2014
(2) British Bankers Association Press Release, Small Business Support, Q4 2013
(3) CDFA, Inside Community Finance, 2013
(4) NESTA, The Rise of Future Finance Benchmarking Report, 2013
(5) Company websites and author estimates

funding role (notably the overdraft). At first, term debt was normally provided by a structured loan. However, in the last 20 years retail banks have supplied commercial mortgages as well. In most major industrialised countries these lenders may often account for about 60% of total supply. In the UK measured as a percentage of the stock of loans outstanding, it was just below this level in December 2013.

Loans from banks with a money transmission relationship with a firm rely very heavily on relationship knowledge gained through the wider banking activities to gain information to help reduce the risk to the lender of making a lending decision. Also, the money transmission relationship a bank has with a customer can subsequently be used to monitor post-loan drawn-down activities by the management team. Lending agreements may well include covenants about the operation of the bank account as a condition of the deal.

Other financial institutions (banks, mutual societies, other financial institutions)

Over the last 20 years and especially since the turn of the millennium, an increasing proportion of smaller-business term debt has been available from financial institutions that do not supply the money transmission account to the firm. In part, stronger competition for the supply of funds to mid-market and larger corporate businesses has encouraged some specialist banks (some times called 'merchant banks') to move into the smaller firm market. At the same time, regulatory reform has encouraged more cross-border lending; for example, German or French-owned banks could agree loans to UK firms, or vice versa. Regulatory reform also allowed many mutual building societies in the UK to turn into banks or start to supply commercial mortgages. At the end of 2013, non-retail bank suppliers contributed nearly 40% of all structured loan facilities to small firms (it was an even higher share a few years earlier).

As a result of these developments, many smaller firms now may have a term debt product from a bank that does not supply its money transmission services. The lack of access to the information provided in the current account does influence the way a lender assesses both the credit information and monitors a loan. Non-retail bank facilities of this type are often called 'stand-alone' rather than 'relationship' loans. They will nearly always be fully secured for better quality customers. Non-retail bank suppliers look to identify strong expanding firms in the market and offer them a bespoke product. Targeting customers this way will keep down risk and costs overall, leading to competitive pricing.

Fewer differences are evident for commercial mortgages between the different types of supplier. For both retail and other financial intuitions these are fully secured products. However, the 'stand-alone' versus 'relationship' distinction drawn above may still be relevant especially in times of financial distress.

Peer-to-peer lending and crowdfunding

Especially since the onset of the global financial crisis in 2007/8 much has been made in both the USA and the UK about the growth in peer-to-peer (P2P) lending and crowdfunding. In the provision of term debt this wholly covers the provision of term loans, often of shorter duration of one to three years and rarely longer. It does not as yet include a commercial mortgage (though some providers are starting to explore this route as well). The key feature is the exclusion of a bank or any other mainstream financial institution from the supply process. Traditionally, someone with cash to save would deposit the funds with a bank that are then on-lent to a business. In P2P lending the saver lends direct to the business. The objective is a better rate of deposit interest return than saving with a bank (in effect, a P2P lending has access to the banks' margin between interest paid on deposits and charged on loans).

P2P lending in reality has been around in a modest way for generations, notably in the form of corporate loans from one firm to another. This is not commonplace but does exist in most countries. These loans are often linked to investment projects to build new plant or facilities in order to fulfil a contract between the two firms. So a car manufacturer may well provide a loan to a parts supplier to fund a new production facility and then place an order to consume the goods produced.

However, the enhanced attention to P2P in recent years is the result of crowdfunding. This is where an internet-based investment platform has been developed to link willing investors and borrowers together to allow them to strike a deal. The crowdfunding platform goes some way to address the asymmetric information issues in the market. The platform provides a shop window for firms to advertise what they need the money for and other information, Also, a 'crowd' of investors can each lend the same business a small sum that combines to a larger amount via an aggregation service operated by the platform (which also collects repayments and interest). With careful selection and lower costs both sides believe they get a good deal, mainly as they have cut out the middleman (the bank manager). The market has grown rapidly over the last few years from small beginnings in both the USA and the UK in particular. However, as a share of total loan facilities outstanding for small firms it still only represents a small percentage of the market (it has a bigger role in the gross supply of loans). For smaller amounts of funding over shorter terms crowdfunding increasingly provides a real alternative to more traditional sources of debt funding.

CONCLUSION

A majority of firms use some form of debt funding over a business lifecycle and for entrepreneurial firms especially this will include structured debt in the form of term loans and commercial mortgages.

The majority of applications for loans and commercial mortgages are successful especially for established firms who have borrowed before. However, more difficult conditions have always been evident for newer firms. Many firms may be able to increase changes of successfully accessing these finance types by looking at themselves through the eye of a potential lender.

Crowdfunding methods based on internet-based platforms have become very popular in the last few years in a number of countries. In reality P2P business lending has been available for generations but new technology has made it more accessible and lower risk for all concerned. Smaller firms now have a real alternative to bank-sourced debt funding.

BIBLIOGRAPHY

BERGER, A.N. and UDELL, G.F. Small Firms and Debt Finance. In ACS, Z.J. and AUDRETSCH D.B. (eds.) *Handbook of Entrepreneurship Research*, 1st Ed., Boston, Kluwer Academic Publishers, 2003 (reprinted 2005).

HUGHES, A. and STOREY, D.J. (eds.) *Finance and the Small Firm*, London, Routledge, 1994.

NESTA *The Rise of Future Finance: The Alternative Funding Benchmark Report 2013*, London, NESTA, 2014.

STIGLITZ, J.E. and WEISS, A.M. Credit rationing in markets with incomplete information, *American Economic Review*, 71, pp. 393–410, 1981.

STIGLITZ, J. E and WEISS, A. Credit Rationing and Collateral. In EDWARDS, J., FRANKS, J., MAYER, C. and SCHAEFER, S. (eds.) *Recent Developments in Corporate Finance*, Cambridge, Cambridge University Press, 1986.

DATA SOURCES

Regular data on loans and commercial mortgages to UK SMEs can be accessed from the British Bankers Association (BBA) and the Bank of England.

For the BBA press releases *Support for Small Firms*: www.bba.org.uk/news/statistics/sme-statistics/ (accessed 10 July 2014).

For the Bank of England Bankstats database: www.bankofengland.co.uk/statistics/Pages/bankstats/default.aspx (accessed 10July 2014).

Chapter 5

Cash-flow products: overdraft and business credit cards

Term loans and commercial mortgages are both used on a discretionary basis as they should be linked to entrepreneurial activity. However, many business owners seek to do no more than operate a successful business on a day-to-day basis. This is an extremely valuable objective and often still difficult to do well. Moreover, quite unfairly, business owners who make this choice are often seen as lacking ambition.

However, as discussed in Chapter 1, all businesses have no choice but to consider cash-flow finance. The need to balance the books in cash-flow terms is a key business skill. Moreover, the financial products most used by owners to help achieve this goal are debt-based. They are the business overdraft and the business credit card. (Firms may use a trade account as well, a form of non-bank debt finance.) Other financial products to support this activity that are not debt-based are discussed in Chapter 6, although these tend to be more suitable for firms with more complex cash-flow funding requirements.

MORE ABOUT CASH-FLOW FUNDING

The need to balance the books of a business on a day-to-day basis to ensure debts are paid as they fall due summarises well the key elements of cash-flow funding. For large numbers of smaller firms, cash-flow funding needs are normally quite modest. In such circumstances, cash-flow management can comprise a mixture of:

- The retention and maintenance of a core capital base of reserves in the balance sheet sufficient to meet any trading shortfall for a period of time. Various views abound on how large the reserves need to be (too much could be seen as 'wasteful'). However, it should really be linked to the type of business involved. Ideally, reserves to fund either one complete stock cycle or pay all input costs for a period of time provide good protection from a short-term cash-flow problem. (Funding for other equivalent elements of business activity may be more appropriate, depending on industry.) This is a matter for the judgement of the owners' and financial advisers. The key point is that the business was sufficiently capitalised at the start with founder equity and this has been added to and maintained as the business has grown, even if this growth is modest over many years. Some of the profits have been retained in the firm, rather than drawn as dividends or earnings.

- Careful management of the firms' net trade position. Firms give and receive trade credit as a way of doing business. Where possible, credit given and credit received should be kept in proportion to one another. For many firms, especially in the service sector, this is possible especially if value-add is high and material input costs are low. Firms that have more entrenched cash-flow management issues can use complex products, as discussed in Chapter 6.
- The use of a short-term credit facility linked to the firms' current account (which is used to make and receive transactions) or an equivalent stand-alone credit facility (such as a credit card).

The majority of firms do not have significant and strategic cash-flow management problems so do not need specialised products beyond some way of financing the stock on the shelves – or goods in the factory – waiting to be sold and sales revenue generated but not yet paid for by the purchaser. Rather, managing cash-flow is one of the many daily problems the business owners need to handle. For these firms, the combination of various management practices such as holding cash reserves in the business and closely managing creditors and debtors is often sufficient. If required, firms may use short-term credit facilities as well. A range of financial products are available to address this cash-flow funding requirement.

Overdrafts

An overdraft facility linked to a business current account accurately describes the key features of this funding product. The current account provided by a bank is a money transmission product to send and receive funds either in cash, cheque or a range of different forms of electronic payments. It is a core element of the accounting and purchasing arrangements in any business. An overdraft facility simply is an agreement by the bank to allow the customer to make payments from the account, even though they do not have sufficient funds to pay the bill, so the account is overdrawn. The overdraft limit used can fluctuate up and down daily, based upon funds being credited into and paid out of the money transmission account. The expectation of the bank is that this lack of sufficient funds is a temporary shortfall until money owed to the business is received into the account and it will go back into a positive balance.

The alternative description for an overdraft in some countries is a line of credit. In many instances, the two terms 'overdraft' and 'line of credit' are interchangeable. However, one distinction is that it is possible to have a credit facility on a line of credit without a direct link to the money transmission system. Rather, it is opened with a zero balance that can move into a negative position. Money is transferred in on settlement days to clear the negative balance. In larger firms, a similar arrangement might be called a committed money line with, again, the lack of a direct link to the money transmission system. Overdraft facilities are nearly always unsecured borrowing. However, in practical terms small business owners would be required to give a personal guarantee in order to obtain the overdraft facility.

Until recently, the regulatory regime for overdrafts made this product fairly simple to set up and a flexible source of funding for small firms. Many business owners did a lot of external funding this way, even for other than strictly cash-flow-based reasons. The last decade in particular has seen a return to a greater enforcement of the distinction between appropriate funding with most banks now keen to ensure overdrafts only really cover cash-flow shortfalls on day-to-day. Regulatory changes have reinforced this trend. As a result, even before the onset of the financial crisis in 2007, overdraft usage in the UK was in long-term decline. However, this structural change in the overall market for overdrafts should not be confused with the value that many firms still attach to having a overdraft facility; this is unlikely to change very much in the medium to long term.

Business credit cards

It is often not realised that a business credit card and an overdraft have much in common. At first glance, the two financial products look different. Of course, rather than a credit card, it is a business debit card that links the ability to make purchases using point of sale or mobile technology to an existing current account (which may have an overdraft facility). However, a more detailed review indicates in practical terms both the overdraft and a credit card add a borrowing facility to an account primarily set up to make and receive payments.

A credit card is a wholly separate product with its own financial limit sitting outside the firm's current account. The only link to a current account may well be the monthly funds transfer for the purposes of settlement. For many firms, a credit card effectively provides a competing service to the current account with an overdraft. The difference between the two products is that interest on an overdraft is calculated on a daily basis from the first day an account facility is available (even if not used, a fee is charged for the facility). In contrast, in the case of a credit card, if the monthly purchases are paid in full on the date agreed with the provider – normally in the middle of the following month – no interest is paid by the user and the credit card provider is paid by the supplier of the goods or service via a fee. If managed correctly, a business credit card offers a free overdraft for up to 50 plus days (from the start of day one in the reference month to the settlement day in the middle of month two). On the other hand, if the business does not have enough funds to pay off the card bill, short-term credit is extended and interest is charged as well. Interest is then paid until the balance is repaid.

As reviewed in Chapter 3, based on the latest UK data, the credit card is now the single most used credit product in the small-business sector. Many firms operate day-to-day without an overdraft by using a credit card. As a result, overdraft usage is increasingly concentrated amongst a smaller group of firms with more substantial cash-flow needs (generally speaking, credit card limits are lower than overdrafts). This change is also another factor behind the long-term decline in total overdraft use by small firms.

Trade accounts

In the days before widespread availability of a business credit card, many firms offered a monthly account for customers. This was quite common practice amongst firms of all sizes until the 1970s and 1980s; often these facilities were offered on trust and on interest-free terms. It was not uncommon, for example, for a local builder with a number of vehicles to have a petrol account at the local garage that was settled at the end of the month. Alternatively, the high street butcher may well have a similar arrangement with the hotel to supply fresh meat every day of the week. Traditionally, the trust came from the local arrangement and that the purchaser was a larger firm with a 'good' reputation.

In most cases, these types of facility have become much less common in the small-business community especially. In effect, these arrangements allowed one firm to subsidise the cash-flow management costs of a customer in an effort to secure loyalty. As well as using a credit card, small firms have generally moved to a single invoice or direct purchase arrangement, where settlement terms are agreed in the contract with an invoice being sent following delivery of the goods. It is now more likely that a hotel chain will have a national contract for wholesale meat supply rather than buying local in small amounts. Credit accounts do continue in certain industries such as builders merchants, which are typically chain-operated by larger firms supplying smaller builders. The credit facilities are now also on a firm legal footing with proper credit management facilities.

Another alternative is the use of an affinity-linked credit card. This is discussed in more detail in the section on supply, 'Affinity and trade card issuers'.

WHAT SORT OF FIRMS USE OVERDRAFTS AND CREDIT CARDS?

The vast majority of firms need a modest amount of cash-flow support at some point during a typical business lifespan. For some firms, this may be a fairly regular occurrence; for others, it is less frequent. As a result, around 60–75% of all firms in most Organization for Economic Co-operation and Development (OECD) markets have at least an overdraft facility or a credit card. This is in line with the situation in the UK. Many firms have both as they are used to cover the cash-flow funding needs of different aspects of operations (an overdraft to pay for raw materials and wages and a credit card to fund travel costs by the sales force). Of course, actually having access to the product does not mean all firms are using these products at the same time. Typically, under half of all overdraft facilities are being used at the end of a monthly trading period with many firms dipping into and out of a negative facility on a daily basis. Credit cards have a rolling facility as well but tend to have a more regular usage pattern linked to the interest-free period on purchases. Most firms build up a debt, allowing payments from sales receipts to accumulate in a current account, which, in turn, are used to repay the card bill in full before any monthly interest is charged (Tables 5.1 and 5.2).

An often discussed question when an overdraft is granted is how long does the bank expect the account to be overdrawn and by how much? The overdraft probably originally started as a financial arrangement between farmers and merchants to cover the seasonal pattern of payments over a crop cycle. In the case

Table 5.1 *Users of Business Overdrafts in the UK, 2013*

		By Employment Size-band			
Percentages	*All SMEs*	*0*	*1–9*	*10–49*	*50–249*
Use	18	15	25	29	28
Applied	6	4	12	13	11
*Successful**	73	67	79	91	95

Source: SME Finance Monitor, Q42013 Report, tables pages 47, 69 and 116

* To boost sample sizes, these are 18 month rates ending Q3, 2013.

Table 5.2 *Users of Business Credit Cards in the UK, 2013*

		By Employment Size-band			
Percentages	*All SMEs*	*0*	*1–9*	*10–49*	*50–249*
With a card	18	15	23	37	49

Source: SME Finance Monitor, Q42013 Report, tables page 47

* To boost sample sizes, these are 18 month rates ending Q3, 2013.

of some industries this pattern of usage may still be appropriate with a view to the account moving into credit at the end of the season as goods are sold. In most sectors, the cycle may be shorter, perhaps within a calendar month, or a quarterly pattern linked to the delivery of a tranche of orders. So a small firm may need to buy in raw materials using trade credit at the start of the month but will need to fund a wage bill in the middle of the month, creating the need for an overdraft until invoices are paid. The point to stress is that each business will have its own internal pattern, often similar to firms in the same industry. This also re-emphasises the link between overdraft usage and the money transmission activities of the firm.

The same points can also be made regarding the size of the overdraft or credit card limit. Firms agree a limit with the supplier to meet the projected maximum need of the business with a bit of headroom to spare. If this limit is exceeded, the bank or card provider could refuse to make payments to suppliers, so impacting on a business's credit rating or stopping wage payments. Normally this would be a last resort after a number of warnings. A more typical outcome for an overdraft at least is that if a business exceeds its limit, the bank will increase the interest rate on the facility.

SUCCESS FACTORS IN OVERDRAFT AND CREDIT CARD APPLICATIONS

All decisions to agree credit facilities have common aspects but in most cases now overdraft and credit card applications are more automated and less subjective decisions than for structured debt products. It is quite common for applications and decisions for cash-flow products to be made and received online in a semi-automated way. However, by understanding the process, business owners can raise the likelihood of a successful application (Figures 5.1 and 5.2).

In considering an application for an overdraft or a credit card, a small firm should particularly review a few key areas.

The business current account

As the majority of applications are automatically assessed by a potential supplier, much of this will be based on the information in the current account. In many cases, this data will already be held by the current account supplier (who typically would be able to offer both products). Alternatively, in the case of a new supplier being approached, information-sharing arrangements are in place to allow credit card companies to have access to key data elements of a current account direct from a bank (or a new current account or credit card supplier can just ask to see copies of old statements from the previous supplier).

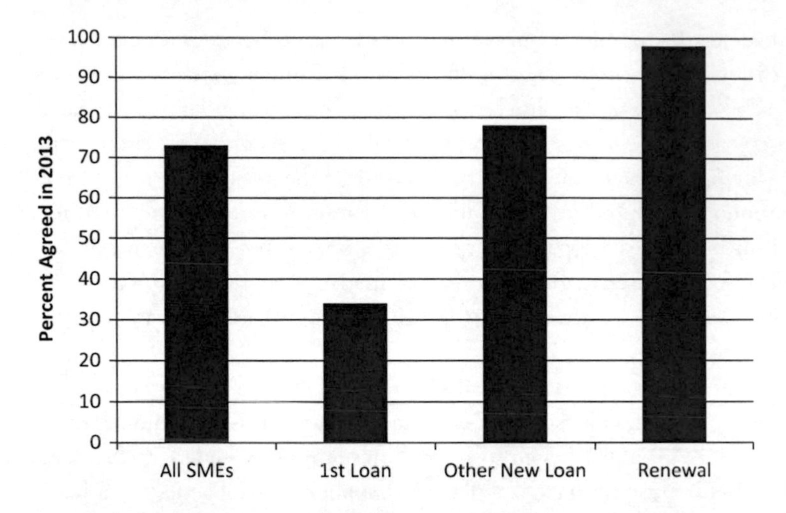

Figure 5.1
Overdraft acceptance rate – by type of application

Source: SMEFM Q4 2013, see table 4.3

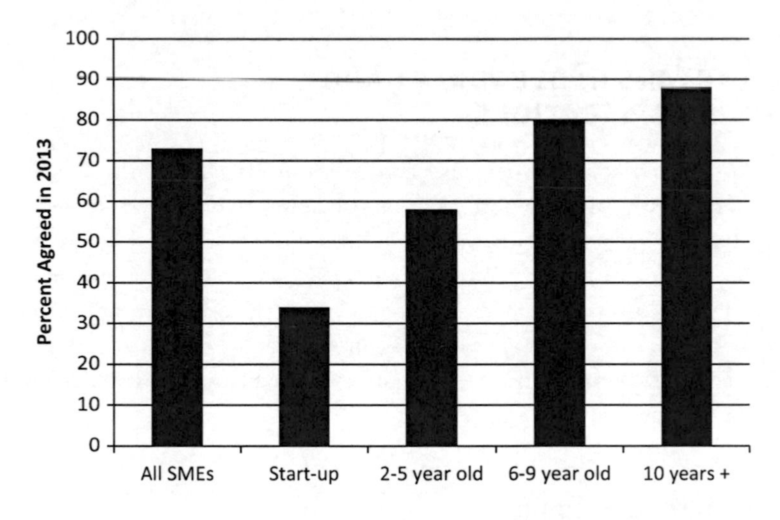

Figure 5.2
Overdraft acceptance rate – by business age

Source: SMEFM Q4 2013, see table 4.3

Any short-term credit provider will be looking for evidence of regular receipts of income (how much and how often) to judge the scale and maturity of the business. At the same time, the assessment will also consider 'account misbehaviour' such as regular bounced cheques, particularly with a common pattern (such as every Friday as the wages are drawn). In some cases as well, a supplier will review how much a business has left in its accounts at the end of the month as a proxy for profitability. A common problem is created if firms make and receive cash payments and purchases with only the net difference put into the current account (if at all).

The detailed review of patterns of behaviour in a current account provides a forensic DNA of a business from day-to-day. If a business has any unusual 'events' in the year before an application (especially the last three months) it is sensible to tell the bank or card company making the assessment about it or expect a challenge back. This will often be done by reviewing the behaviour of the applicant's account with a comparable group of firms.

The personal finances of the owner–manager

While many small business owners keep business and personal financial activities entirely separate, the majority do not. In the case of an overdraft application, it would look odd to a supplier if a business was regularly transferring cash into the business from the applicant's personal resources as this may well indicate the business is weaker than it may first appear. It could indicate other things such as banking cash payments into a personal facility and then moving the funds to the business (which is done by some firms to avoid higher fees for banking cash in a branch for a business customer). In the case of credit card applications, it would be fairly common to check a personal credit score; the concern would be that personal debts will draw too much out of the business rather than be available to repay the business credit card balance.

The applicant's customers

Positive decisions on short-term small-business credit applications do not hinge upon how good a business idea is and if the business has a legally binding contract with its customers. Rather, these are essentially short-term credit facilities to fund the day-to-day needs of an already successful and stable business. As a result, in such circumstances a credit provider will look at the 'quality' of the applicant's customer base.

If a firm applying for an overdraft buys goods for cash two days a week and sells them at auction three days a week and the auction house settles bills 30 days after the sale, the ability of the applicant to settle the overdraft will depend on the financial standing of the auction house. In all cases, short-term credit applications will be treated more favourably when:

- A small firm is primarily selling to a much larger well-known firm or government department (although these customers may well delay payment, they do pay).
- A small firm sells in cash and pays on invoice (making the business cash positive most of the time but with occasional gaps in cash-flow to fill).

Most of these assessments of a firm's customer base are done on industry or sectorial assumptions by suppliers (but can be done on a case-by-case basis for special cases).

Why does the business need the facility?

A start-up or growing firm should ideally build the initial cash-flow assumptions into the overall funding needs of a venture; this may well require some pre-revenue funding. Established firms on the other hand can use cash-flow finance to cover day-to-day funding needs. Especially if an application decision is delayed for additional scrutiny, it could be just to find out why the business is applying now when it has not had a facility before. Suppliers are conscious that overdraft and card debt can be used for more entrepreneurial purposes and are seen by small firms as easier forms of credit to access.

WHO ARE THE SUPPLIERS OF OVERDRAFT AND CREDIT CARDS?

Overdraft and credit card suppliers fall into a number of distinct groups.

Retail or high street banks

The direct link between the business current account and a related overdraft facility makes it inevitable that the main retail or high street banks are the only providers of overdraft facilities. For many years the overdraft was regarded as a facility offered to long-standing customers as a courtesy. However, particularly in the last decade, the overdraft is now a product managed separately from the money transmission elements of a current account (Table 5.3).

Less appreciated is that in many markets retail banks are also major suppliers of credit cards to the business sector as well. The ability to generate a whole customer view drawing on current account and wider financial data is a major synergy. From the point of view of the customer as well, use of a current account normally allows them to access a relationship manager to talk to about day-to-day banking issues. This can be helpful in explaining issues or potential problems with a credit record as well. The collection of local data can be used by a relationship manager to ensure any application is done at pace and where needed has got his or her support.

The disadvantages of this arrangement are that firms have to pay for a current account that costs them monthly fees. Some small business owners will also deliberately make separate arrangements from a credit card provider to keep it independent from the bank.

Table 5.3 *Supply of Cash-flow Finance in the UK, 2013*

	Limits (year-end)		*Utilisation (Average over year)*
	Number	*£ bn*	*Percentage*
Overdrafts – high street banks	750,000	22	55%
Other overdrafts	70,000	3	80%
Card issuers – cards in operation	980,000	10	15%
Total	1,800,000	35	46%

Sources
(1) Bank of England, Bankstats, Table A8.1, May 2014
(2) British Bankers Association Press Release, Small Business Support, Q4 2013
(3) SME Finance Monitor, Q42013 Report, tables page 47
(4) Company websites and author estimates

Stand-alone credit card issuers

A separate range of financial institutions have also been set up to issue and operate credit cards both for personal and business customers. Some of them are household names such as American Express. They do not offer a current account or a retail branch network and a relationship manager (although some firms operate a national sales force). It is not uncommon for small-business owners to hold a business credit card separate from its main current account provider. Very often these card issuers target certain types of business credit card user rather than the whole small-business sector. This may typically be high net worth business owners or frequent business travellers as two common examples. In other cases, the service may be based around professionals in business such as engineers, accountants or lawyers. In all cases, these firms are more likely to rely on automated credit decision systems but often have significant associated loyalty schemes (which makes like-for-like price comparison difficult) (Figure 5.3).

Affinity and trade card issuers

Although a business credit card as a financial product for small firms was almost non-existent 30 years ago, thousands of firms offered a monthly charge account. While these monthly accounts are less common now, except in certain industries, affinity cards have been developed to offer an alternative. In most cases, such as the store card in the consumer market, the card is linked to a particular purchasing activity or site.

The best-known examples are the fuel cards offered by major petrol retailers or charge cards offered by DIY chains. Initially, these were offered to executives of larger firms to help them and their employers control spending but over the last decade these have moved to be available to small firms (although sometimes they will exclude sole traders or self-employed from eligibility). In reality, these credit cards are not actually issued by the businesses who market them. Rather, they have a tie-in with a major stand-alone card issuer who is effectively seeking access to a new potential group of customers linked to a single purchasing activity or site. Consequently, assessment techniques are normally virtually the same as in the case of a credit card, although interest rates charged are typically a bit higher. This is because the customer group targeted is still less selective than in mainstream credit card operations, so losses are higher as well (Figure 5.4).

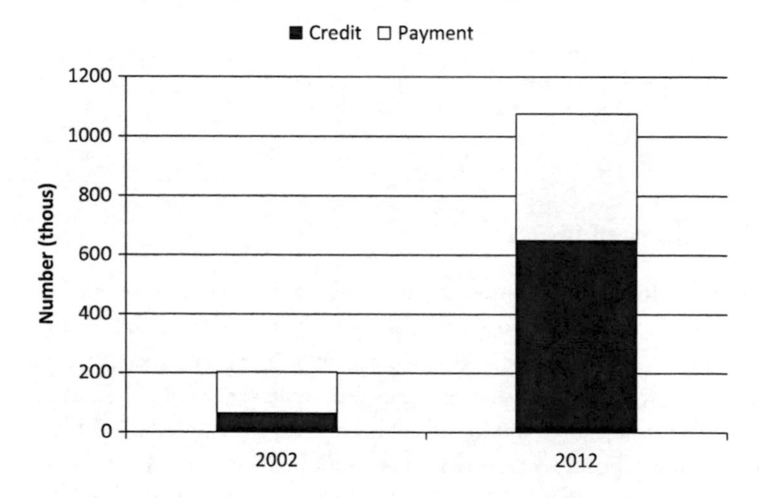

Figure 5.3
Business credit and payment cards

Source: Payments Council, UK Payments Statistics, 2013

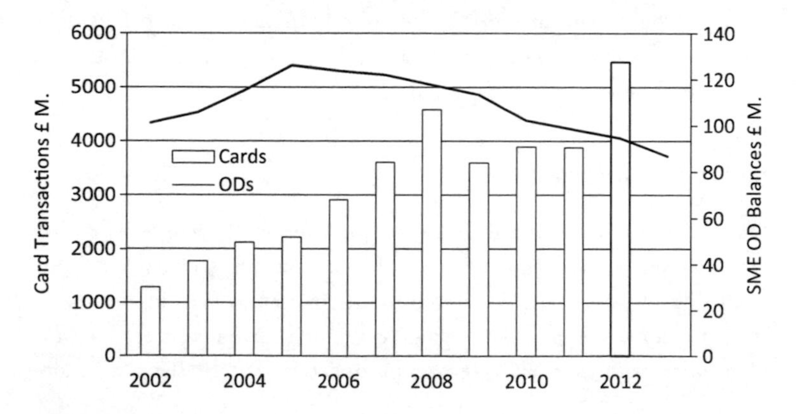

Figure 5.4
SME Overdrafts and Card Transactions

CONCLUSION

Most firms cope with cash-flow finance problems on a day-to-day basis through the use of reserves in the business and the active management of creditor and debtor payments. However, the majority of small firms still have a dedicated cash-flow product in either an overdraft or a credit card. How often these products are used will vary considerably amongst firms but having a facility to use these products is the norm in most small firms.

A number of suppliers offer these cash-flow products. The linkage between an overdraft and a current account has put a limit on the number of overdraft suppliers for many years. However, the growing use of the business credit card, which can be offered as a stand-alone product, has been the key development over the last decade. This has led to new suppliers entering the market and a shift of credit supplied from overdraft to card-based sources.

For some businesses, cash-flow management is a more significant structural problem. While these firms can, of course, also adopt the management methods discussed above, and use an overdraft or a credit card, in many cases they also benefit from using a specialised financial product range to support invoice finance.

BIBLIOGRAPHY

HUGHES, A. and STOREY, D.J. (eds.) *Finance and the Small Firm*, London, Routledge, 1994.

PAYMENTS COUNCIL *Payments in Focus – Business Payments*, London, Payments Council, 2010.

PAYMENTS COUNCIL *UK Payment Markets*, London, Payments Council, 2013.

PAYMENTS COUNCIL *UK Payment Statistics 2013*, London, Payments Council, 2014.

DATA SOURCES

Regular data on overdrafts used by UK SMEs can be accessed from the British Bankers Association (BBA) and the Bank of England.

For the BBA press releases *Support for Small Firms*: www.bba.org.uk/news/statistics/sme-statistics/ (accessed 10 July 2014).

For the Bank of England Bankstats database: www.bankofengland.co.uk/statistics/pages/bankstats/default.aspx (accessed 10 July 2014).

Credit card and payments data is available from the UK Cards Association and the Payments Council: www.theukcardsassociation.org.uk/2014-facts-figures/index.asp and www.paymentscouncil.org.uk/ (accessed 10 July 2014).

Chapter 6

Factoring and invoice discounting

Overdraft and commercial credit cards are not the only types of financial products available to help firms manage cash-flow. A range of products collectively called factoring and invoice discounting are also available to support this goal. In summary, these products offer a mixture of onward sale and loan options to support cash-flow management. In many cases they are most applicable to firms that have enhanced cash-flow requirements over and above that typically faced by a small firm. Normally, these enhanced requirements are a consequence of the business sector and the stage of enterprise growth. In contrast, use of these products in a number of sectors is very low or even non-existent.

ASSET-BASED FINANCE PRODUCTS

Factoring and invoice discounting are often treated as the same product or confused with one another. However, while both are based on the value of assets tied up within a payments chain, they are very different products with a similar outcome in terms of unlocking these funds for use by the business.

Factoring

Factoring is a financial product that allows successful firms with invoiced orders to gain access to these sales revenues before the date for payment agreed with the customer. This is achieved by selling the rights to this expected income stream to a third party (the factor). When the settlement date for the debt falls, the third party receives the money directly from the customer.

It is worth noting that in many ways factoring is similar to a credit card. In factoring, the seller supplies goods and agrees payment at some future point with the buyer. However, rather than wait until then, the seller gets access to this income early through a factor in return for a fee. In the case of a credit card, a seller supplies goods and receives immediate payment from a card company but allows the buyer to delay payment to a future date in return for a fee.

Although a number of variants to factoring have been developed, at its core this product pays the user immediately a percentage of the value of all invoices reported to the factor. In return the user assigns the rights to receive payment on the invoices from itself to the factor. The advances can be in excess of 90% of the invoiced value but 80–85% is more commonly paid to the user on the sale of the goods. The remaining balance of value in the invoice is held back by the factor and paid over to the user when the invoice is paid by the firm to which goods have been supplied (say at the end of a 30 or 60-day term). The factor will deduct its fee for the service from this balancing payment. Typically, the advance payments are made on a rolling basis to a user as sales invoices are generated and this becomes the cash-flow income for the firm. The adjusted balancing payment is made on a monthly basis for accounts received in the last 30 days.

The variants to this basic factoring product mainly concern the treatment of bad debts, in particular, will any adjustment be made to the balancing charge in the event of the non-payment or late payment of invoices. When factoring is done on a 'non-recourse' basis, the factor has to take on the full cost of bad debts not the user. Less common is a 'recourse' arrangement where the balancing payment is reduced to account for some or all the bad debts (although the factor may offer the user an insurance policy to cover this as well to offset the reduction in the balancing payment). Another variant is 'forfaiting' mainly used in export markets where a firm sells rights to an individual transaction (rather than all or part of its accounts receivables for a period of time).

Another generic feature of all types of factoring is the way a factor manages the client's invoice and collection arrangements. This is considerably more than a tie-in via the internet or electronic systems between the factor and user just to transmit information and payments. Rather, as the factor has bought the rights to the invoice receivables of a user, it is responsible for the administration and collection of these receivables. This includes all ongoing administrative and legal duties such as chasing and enforcing bad debts. In part, this activity offers significant overhead costs savings for the user as the services do not need to be replicated. The user will not have to employ administrative staff to do this work (or fewer of them). The cost of this activity is part of the fee for the overall service but factoring operations will also benefit from significant economies of scale in undertaking this work.

Invoice discounting

Invoice discounting is a debt product where a user obtains a loan based on the value of the money due to be paid in the future by its customers. Unlike factoring, the ownership of the rights to the debt stay with the user and are not transferred.

Rather, the accounts receivable act as the security for the loan and they are often formally legally assigned to the discounter to enhance this role. Unlike an overdraft, invoice discounting has no link to a business current account.

In invoice discounting, the key feature is that a user is allowed to draw down a percentage of its outstanding sales invoices on a rolling basis. This figure will change on a daily basis as goods are sold or payments are received. The discounter typically charges a monthly fee for this service (say 0.75% of the outstanding invoices) and interest on the actual money advanced. Normally, the discounter will seek a fixed charge or assignment over the book debts to provide security as well.

On top of invoice discounting being a loan, the other main difference from factoring concerns the confidentiality of the service. In the case of factoring, as the legal right to ownership of the debt is acquired by the factor, the customers of the user have to be advised that payment should be made to the factor directly and not to the supplier (the user of the factoring service). In contrast, this is not needed in the case of invoice discounting. Most invoice discounting tends to be on a confidential basis but a disclosed service can be used.

In addition, invoice discounting offers none of the possible administrative savings in terms of invoice billing and collection available in factoring. The user retains ownership of the sums due from invoices and must do all the work required to collect the revenue. Indeed, users of invoice discounting may well be required to have more substantial accounting resources than users of factoring. Invoice discounting requires an almost daily calculation of the value of accounts receivable adjusted for sales receipts and payments in and out on a rolling basis. The discounter will seek evidence that these arrangements are in place and may well ask for access to relevant on line systems to monitor the position and funds draw down. Factoring is the sale of invoices to a third party that once passed on to the factor becomes its responsibility.

As in the case of factoring, the treatment of bad debts in discounting can vary as well. It is possible to have, in effect, 'non-recourse' invoice discounting normally through an insurance-based add-on to the basic service; without it, if a customer defaults and does not pay the subsequent bad debt would be written off leaving a firm to suffer both the loss of the debt and a reduction in its accounts receivable used to draw down a loan. An insurance product, in effect, pays out on the bad debt and offsets the loan drawn against the accounts receivable.

WHO USES FACTORING AND INVOICE DISCOUNTING?

The similarity between factoring and the way a credit card operates has already been noted. More generally, both factoring and invoice discounting provide an enhanced product range to manage cash-flow, especially over and above an overdraft. However, both alternative ways of funding cash-flow are not necessarily cheaper than an overdraft or a credit card. Indeed, some commentators will argue that the range of fees and charges could make both types of asset finance more expensive than on an overdraft or a credit card; other commentators will note that factoring especially may save a firm a lot of overhead costs. The choice to use these specialised products is rarely about price. As a result, it is worth considering the key features that make them attractive to some types of business but not others (Table 6.1).

In this regard, it is worth remembering that both overdraft and credit cards are linked mainly to the historical performance or current business needs of a commercial venture. Established firms with well-understood trends in cash-flow or patterns of credit card behaviour find it fairly easy to obtain cash-flow facilities. However, if a business is in an expanding market the underlying cash-flow needs are still not fully known. Both factoring and invoice discounting automatically fund cash-flow requirements in parallel with business growth and can be regarded as being linked to the forward-looking potential of a business. The same could be achieved by going back every month to a bank and asking for an increase in an overdraft limit to match the growth of the firm. However, each time this would involve additional time and transaction costs. Hence, fairly rapidly growing firms tend to be attracted to factoring and invoice discounting.

In addition, overdrafts and credit cards best suit established firms that dip in to negative credit balances for short periods of time on a fairly predictable basis. The typical monthly pattern of activity might be that the business has some ongoing savings in its current account held over from month to month. However, during the course of the month, as bills fall due or purchases are made, for brief periods of time these reserves are not sufficient. In these circumstances, overdrafts and credit cards help. However, if a business does not have a surplus of cash at the start of the trading period the business could be in negative credit for most of the month and only be in a positive cash position for a few days a month (even though they make a profit). As interest is charged daily, this can be an expensive financing option and, where possible, firms with these characteristics may well be better off looking at asset financing. Often start-up firms are seen as likely to see these products as useful but normally a factor or invoice discounter will need a minimum trading period and debtor book value before agreeing a facility. However, for a larger group of growing young enterprises that have moved successfully past immediate start-up, the attraction of these products is high (especially if they have modest cash reserves to fund an expanding cash-flow) (Table 6.2 and Figure 6.1).

Table 6.1 *Users of Factoring and Invoice Discounting in the UK, 2013*

		By Employment Size-band			
Percentages	*All SMEs*	*0*	*1–9*	*10–49*	*50–249*
Use either	2	1	4	10	17

Source: SME Finance Monitor, Q42013 Report, tables pages 47

Table 6.2 *Number of Users of Asset-Based Finance by Product Group in the UK, 2013*

Product Type	*Clients (no.)*	*Turnover (£m)*	*Avg. Turnover (£)*
Domestic Factoring	18,129	18,569	1,024,271
Domestic Invoice Discounting	19,013	238,602	12,549,414
Other – mainly Export linked	6,343	18,280	2,881,917
Total	43,485	275,451	6,334,391

Source: ABFA, Quarterly Statistics, Q4 2013. Note data includes 700 non-SMEs

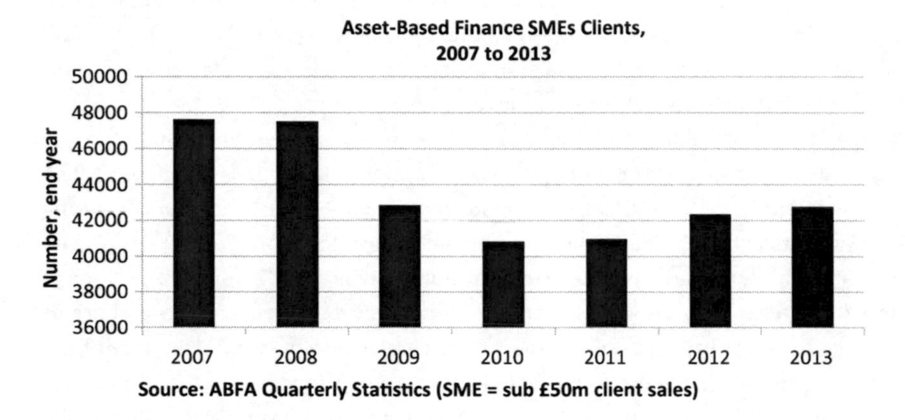

Figure 6.1
Number of SME Users, 2013

Asset finance does not suit all business types. Very few industry types are totally excluded from using these products. Rather, any problems are more likely to be linked to a firm's customer base. Self-evidently, largely cash-based operations are not eligible (where in effect the personal credit card substitutes for factoring) and generally firms dominated by business to consumer transactions are not seen as suitable. Factoring firms are especially uncomfortable with the prospect of chasing up debts owed by private individuals. Consequently, most customers using these asset-based funding such factoring products are in manufacturing, wholesaling and a range of business to business services (such as recruitment, printing, courier services and plant hire).

Historically, factoring especially, and, to a lesser extent, invoice discounting have been perceived as products only used by financially weaker and vulnerable firms that had no choice but to use this product. This is far from the truth. Rather, these products are normally used by a particular type of business in a key part of its business lifespan post-start-up and growing. They are also used to address some specific industry considerations. Far from being financially vulnerable, the reporting requirements to use the products are very significant. The suggestion that users are financially vulnerable is probably linked to the attractiveness of this product range to firms that do not have substantial cash reserves to fund dips in cash-flow. However, this does not mean these firms are financially weak or exceptionally risky. Rather, they need to use the appropriate cash-flow product to ensure successful trading.

SUCCESS FACTORS IN FACTORING AND INVOICE DISCOUNTING APPLICATIONS

It is important to remember that all firms using factoring and invoice discounting must be trading successfully to the degree of obtaining a steady stream of invoiced orders to either factor or discount. Beyond that, as well as previous observations regarding sectorial and business life stage considerations, three things will probably help a business secure a good deal for this type of product:

- A minimum level of invoiced sales. In the case of factoring and invoice discounting, sales in excess of £50,000 a year or even £100,000 are typically required. For a factoring operation, traditionally this would appear to be the minimum efficient size in which to set up bespoke invoicing and collection arrangements (although innovation by some suppliers is challenging this requirement – see the section on 'Digital market operators' later in this chapter).
- The quality of the customer base in the applicant firm. Both factors and discounters rely on the certainty of payment against invoice from customers. It is inevitable that the better the quality of the customer base the more attractive a firm will be to a factor or a discounter.
- The strength of the firm's in-house accounting and management systems. This is of course an important consideration for all types of external finance. However, as a third-party finance provider whose source of funds is wholly dependent on how good this information is, it is likely to come under enhanced scrutiny when a new arrangement is sought by a user.

WHO ARE THE SUPPLIERS OF FACTORING AND INVOICE DISCOUNTING SERVICES?

In the aftermath of the 2007–2011 financial crises, a renewed interest has occurred in factoring and invoice discounting. However, it is actually a very old financial

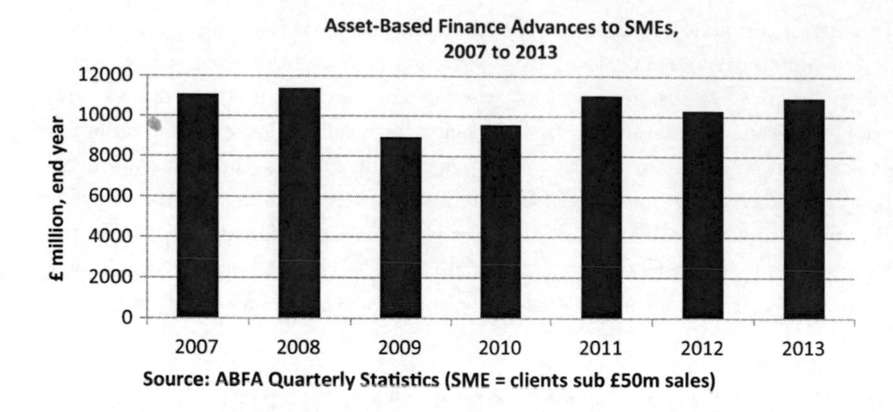

Figure 6.2
SME Client Advances £m, since 2007

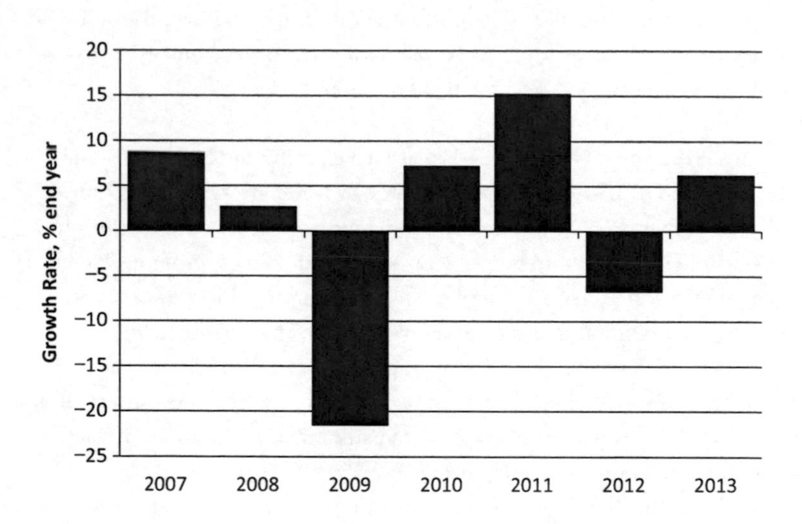

Figure 6.3
SME Client Advances Growth Rate, 2007–2013

service, probably with a history just as long as traditional lending via a bank. The suppliers of these services fall into three groups.

Specialised factoring and invoice discount firms

In the UK market at least, factoring and invoice discounting has a very fragmented supplier base with a significant number of small specialised providers. Very few are household names. Most work in particular sub-sectors of the market. The fragmented nature of the market is mainly the consequence of the involvement of a number of foreign-owned banks and large corporates who have decided to use this product range to develop a UK financial services operation. This has been the preferred way of developing a range of services for small firms, rather than market entry through a money transmission-based operation using high street branches and a current account.

The involvement of large non-financial firms is also especially interesting. In effect, they are moving into a form of supply chain finance helping to fund customers buying and selling on the same firms' mainstream products, For example, a large multinational electronic component manufacturer can sell goods in a semi-manufactured form to another firm for re-manufacture, or build it into a new product. These are then sold by the firm in the middle of the chain to a retailer with an invoice to pay in 60 days. The large multinational at the start of the chain with a strong balance sheet and financial reserves discounts the final invoice allowing the retailer to pay for the goods. Of course, the firm in the middle of the chain receives the sums on invoice and pays for the components it has bought from the multinational in the first place.

High street banks

The high street banks all have factoring and invoice discounting services. However, these activities are noticeably less evident in the UK market as the specialised providers have an enhanced role. Indeed, many of the specialised firms operating in this market obtained wholesale funding for operations from banks. As a result, the high street banks have an indirect involvement in this type of funding as well as direct provision.

Digital market operators

Digital market operators such as Market Invoice in the UK have been a source of innovation in the asset finance sector over the last few years and are increasingly important in this area. They offer a peer-to-peer version of factoring and invoice discounting. For example, a firm that has achieved a successful sale, which includes receipt of payment at some future date, is able to offer this to hundreds of potential investors who will supply some of the funds immediately for a discount or fee. This is done via a digital market place. When the original bill is finally paid, the digital platform receives the funds and pays the investors.

The key difference from the traditional factoring product is the bidding process where the debt is offered to a very large number of investors (with the bidding creating a price). Also, similar to forfaiting, a user firm is able to offer one invoice or a small number of debts to the service; they do not need to offer the whole sales ledger.

These digital platforms are growing rapidly. It could be that the acceptance of this version of factoring especially will lead to a growing acceptance of the product by all types of business. The threshold for the use of asset finance may well fall below £100,000 or even £50,000 invoiced sales in the next few years. Also, some of the stigma and possible embarrassment felt by some owners using this product may well disappear as its acceptance increases in the small-business population.

CONCLUSION

While most firms can use sensible day-to-day management practice, plus a credit card and if needed an overdraft to cope with cash-flow finances, that is not the case for all. Certain types of firms, notably younger and fast-growing operations, as well as firms in a number of core business-to-business sectors, are just as likely to use asset funding, especially factoring and invoice discounting. For many firms, these products offer an easily accessible and cost-effective alternative to a large overdraft alone. Also, for some firms, these products provide the only product range that can effectively meet their specialised cash-flow funding needs.

BIBLIOGRAPHY

BRENNAN, M.J., MAKSIMOVICS, V. and ZECHNER, J. Vendor finance, *The Journal of Finance*, 43 (8), pp. 1127–1141, 1988.

GARCÍA-TERUEL P.J. and MARTÍNEZ-SOLANO, P. Determinants of trade credit: a comparative study of European SMEs, *International Small Business Journal*, 28 (3), pp. 215–233, 2010.

KLAPPER, L. The role of factoring for financing small and medium enterprises, *Journal of Banking and Finance*, 30 (11), pp. 3111–3130, 2006.

PEEL, M.J., WILSON, N. and HOWARTH, C. Late payment and credit management in the small firm sector: some empirical evidence, *International Small Business Journal*, 18 (2), pp. 17–37, 2000.

SOUFANI, K. The role of factoring in financing UK SMEs: a supply side analysis, *Journal of Small Business and Enterprise Development*, 8 (1), pp. 37–46, 2001.

SOUFANI, K. On the determinants of factoring as a financing choice: evidence from the UK, *Journal of Economics and Business*, 54 (2), pp. 239–252, 2002.

DATA SOURCES

Factoring statistics can be found on the UK Asset Based Finance Association website: www.abfa.org.uk/members/statistics.asp (accessed 10 July 2014).

Chapter 7

Leasing

Leasing and asset finance is a type of funding where a business can acquire the use of an item of capital equipment without having to pay the full purchase price upfront. In such an arrangement, a rental agreement is set up between the user of the capital goods (the lessee) and the purchaser and owner of the goods (the lessor). As such, it is potentially a source of funding for both entrepreneurial and cash-flow funding. A business can use leasing to update and replace a fleet of vehicles to keep its sales force on the road. Alternatively, a new venture can use this type of finance to acquire the capital equipment to get production started. In both cases, the initial cash outlay can be reduced, allowing time for the new equipment to be set up and put into operation to generate income to fund repayment. This dual role ensures leasing is one of the most flexible sources of small business funding.

Indeed, in addition to a reduction in the initial capital outlay, the advantages of using leasing as a source of funding are enhanced by corporate tax considerations. The tax regime in most countries allows firms to reduce trading profits to reflect how much a business is spending on buying plant and machinery. This reduction in profits subject to taxation is normally achieved through a combination of a deduction in profits for at least part of the value of the initial purchase price and an annual writing-down allowance to reduce any tax liability in future years as plant is worn out with use over time. Any interest paid on borrowed money also attracts tax relief.

However, many start-ups and expanding firms do not make a profit, or the profits are too low to take full advantage of this concession in a reasonable time. At best the relief can be carried forward to offset against future profits but firms would rather get assistance sooner rather than later. A lease arrangement allows someone else to buy the capital equipment (the lessor) and claim the tax relief. The lessor can then immediately pass on the benefit of the tax concession to the small firm in the price it charges to use the equipment.

LEASING AND OTHER ASSET FINANCE PRODUCTS

The term 'leasing and asset finance' actually refers to a range of rental products with some different features and characteristics. The differences can be significant for the potential user; the most distinct being whether they end up with ownership of the asset at the end of the lease period or they return it to the lessor.

Hire Purchase (HP)

Under an HP agreement the business pays a significant initial deposit to the finance company and starts using the equipment. The deposit required could be up to 20% of the cost. The remaining balance of the full purchase cost is a debt owed to the finance company on which interest is paid as well, normally on a monthly basis. As with repayments on a mortgage, the business's outgoings do not change much month-on-month (especially as most often the interest options are on a fixed rate basis). However, over a long period of time the monthly balance outstanding on the initial purchase price falls. Only when the final payment is made does the business actually own the capital item. As a result, HP provides long-term staged payments before ownership.

Leasing

In a leasing arrangement, to start using the equipment the business is normally only required to pay out a small initial deposit such as three or six month's rent in advance. In contrast to an HP arrangement, at the end of the contract period the business also has a wider range of choices regarding the future use of the equipment. Also, a business should find it easier (though still not easy) to end the rental agreement early if circumstances change and set up a new arrangement. At the end of an HP arrangement, the final payment discharges any outstanding debt on the equipment and ownership transfers automatically to the business from the finance company. In leasing deals, on the other hand, rental agreements are shorter so at the end to secure full ownership the business may well have to pay a substantial final payment. (This is on a par with the upfront payment needed to start an HP deal. Indeed, HP is sometimes called reverse leasing.)

Leasing covers two distinct types of funding arrangements for small firms:

Finance lease

This is a rental agreement to cover the full economic life of the capital equipment. At the end of the rental agreement, although the equipment may still be fully serviceable and in operation, it has no significant resale value. Hence, the user can hand the equipment back to the finance company and start a new agreement with more modern equipment. Alternatively, the business can normally pay a much lower 'peppercorn' rent to continue using the equipment. This rent may well be little more than covering the cost of a maintenance agreement. Finance leases are long-term funding arrangements where the business never actually has to own the asset (although if the old equipment is handed back by a business and a new deal is not requested, some finance companies will offer a sale price to allow full ownership).

Operating lease

This is a rental agreement that is not normally expected to run for the full economic life of the capital equipment. The business has a lease to cover a period of operation. At the end of this pre-agreed time, the equipment still has a resale value. Businesses then have the choice to either hand the equipment back – perhaps start a new lease with updated plant – or purchase the item for the current value for the equipment and obtain full ownership. Payments under an operating lease should be lower as a percentage of the capital value of the equipment than under a finance lease as the finance company has the resale value in the equipment at the end of the agreement period.

The types of business and equipment where leasing is especially popular are discussed in the next section. However, by way of illustration, HP is more commonly used for specialised capital equipment that can be almost bespoke to the user. Finance leases are typically used for office equipment and PCs. Finally, operating leases are commonly used in funding motor vehicles.

WHAT TYPE OF FIRMS USE LEASING FINANCE?

Leasing is a very flexible type of business funding and can help firms obtain new equipment under a range of financial circumstances. However, the use of this type of funding does vary between business size and type. Also, in some cases firms may well have to alter some financial and business practices to gain better access to this type of funding, or use alternative sources of finance (Table 7.1).

Table 7.1 *Users of Leasing and other Asset Finance in the UK, 2013*

		By Employment Size-band			
Percentages	*All SMEs*	*0*	*1–9*	*10–49*	*50–249*
Use either	8	5	12	26	37

Source: SME Finance Monitor, Q42013 Report, tables pages 47

Looking at the decision by a firm to use leasing as the means of funding capital purchase, three main considerations are likely to be important:

- The profit and tax position of the business. As mentioned earlier, if a business is very profitable leasing options will be less attractive. An established profitable business is likely to be able to obtain debt funding on good commercial terms. Also, any capital equipment purchases made will allow the business to reduce taxable profits. In these circumstances, a business will likely want to benefit from the lower cost of outright purchase and the tax benefits available for such capital investment. A start-up or rapidly growing business, on the other hand, may not be making any sufficient profit and may have neither the available cash resources nor the ability to take advantage of these capital business reliefs. It may, however, be able to benefit from the tax treatment of the lease payments themselves. Leasing in these circumstances becomes very attractive.
- The cost of the capital purchase relative to the size of the business can be an important consideration. Even for a business where the tax advantages are minimal leasing can still be attractive in many circumstances, especially if the business has no long-term requirement to ever take ownership. This is because the initial capital outlay to get the equipment delivered in leasing is very low. If the capital goods are very expensive relative to the size of the business operation it may well be a sensible option on grounds of risk management considerations alone for a firm to lease and retain its own funds within the business. Fleet car sales are a good example of why leasing is popular even amongst very large and established firms, especially as maintenance and insurance services tend to be outsourced to the finance company as well. This is an issue for the use of leasing, not HP which needs a higher capital outlay anyway.
- The pace of innovation and change in various product areas is important, especially as this in turn is linked to the resale value of equipment at the end of the rental period. If a business depends on access to the latest technology to sustain its market position and equipment is largely out of date every two or three years then leasing may be attractive. The most common types of equipment that fall into this category are office equipment, photocopies and PCs. In many cases, lease arrangements are linked to a maintenance contract with the equipment manufacturer to provide a complete package.

All these factors work with each other to increase the attractiveness of asset finance. Hence, a start-up business seeking to set up a new, office-based operation is very likely to consider leasing. The profit and tax situation will be such that the firm will find it difficult to use capital allowances. At the same time, the initial capital outlay will be high and the business may want to keep founder capital in reserve and the terms of a traditional bank loan may not be attractive (or even unavailable).

At the other end of the scale of business operation, larger SMEs and mid-corporate firms may well be less likely to use leasing other than for very specific asset classes. This is because various parts of the business are growing at different times so capital spending in one part of the business can be used to reduce the profits made elsewhere in the firms. However, even large firms often lease vehicles on grounds of initial capital outlay and tax efficiency. Also, some very large specialised capital items such as train rolling stock, fleets of aircraft and ships are often lease-funded and subject to extremely complex tax planning arrangements. Indeed, for these specialised items, leasing with no ownership is a distinct advantage (for example, a business may never want to own an old, fuel inefficient fleet of aircraft).

SUCCESS FACTORS IN ASSET FINANCE APPLICATIONS

In terms of a business increasing its chances of securing an offer from a leasing business, it should be recognised that all such funding arrangements are, in effect, fully secured. The business rents and maintains the asset but never owns it until the final payment. From a risk perspective of a finance provider this is closer to deciding to agree to a commercial mortgage than a term loan. However, as discussed in the section later on suppliers, the way that asset finance is sold by providers of the most commonly financed assets for small firms is closer to that of an unsecured loan, especially for smaller capital items with a high incidence of point-of-sale finance. As a result, three main factors appear relevant to a successful application.

The ability to fulfil the rental payments

As long as a business can illustrate a source of income to meet the monthly rental costs and has the deposit, then most applications are successful. To agree an HP or a lease arrangement, the finance provider will be keen to establish the certainty and quality of the income stream being used to support the application. As the asset never belongs to the lessee, the finance provider may well be able to assess applications for funding in a less detailed way than, for example, an overdraft. However, a reassurance on ability to pay will be needed and evidenced.

Even so, greater scope for flexibility over the adequacy of revenue is normally available to an applicant for an asset finance arrangement than for more traditional debt funding because security is more certain. For example, part of the attractiveness for start-ups as users of leasing finance is that the rent on a capital item is often considerably lower than the equivalent loan repayments to purchase outright. As a result, the revenue income needed to cover the rental payments will be lower. Also, in certain cases, a finance company will agree to take rental payments direct from the initial start-up funds of an enterprise in its pre-revenue phase; in effect, the leasing provider will require less of a track record history from an applicant to underpin the revenue forecasts in a business plan. Similar arrangements are also offered to established firms seeking to acquire new equipment or a new production line. These arrangements are often more flexible than for structured debt products (which may offer capital repayment holiday for a few months but the interest payments will be required on the balance).

More general creditworthiness indicators

While asset finance can be used to take delivery of, and start using, quite significant items of equipment, the finance product is very often sold alongside, or as part of, the buying process for the related equipment. The use of point-of-sale finance as a result puts more emphasis on a business's credit score than for other types of entrepreneurial finance.

A credit score allows a wide range of finance providers and other businesses to remotely assess the credit status of a business. It is another way to address the core financier worries about adverse selection and moral hazard discussed in earlier chapters. The main users of a business credit score will be providers of finance for point-of-sale purchases (a bank typically has access to more information on a customer's activity through current account data). In many cases, the primary assessment of an application will be based on a credit score.

Unlike a detailed assessment of a loan applicant, a finance provider will base considerable weight in a credit score history on evidence of regular payments made and managing trade credit. This is often taken as an indication of financial management skill and reliability of performance to underpin a lease or HP plan. In most cases, this replaces any in-depth review of the case. Any businesses seeking to use leasing should really investigate its credit status with external agencies. Firms can check the input data for a credit score with the agency and ensure it is correct. For example, a review of the data may well discover mistakes in the address of the business, or in the name that may lead to a false association with adverse court judgments. Also, errors in basic activities such as filing annual returns to Companies House will be noted on the file and should be addressed. Finally, in some cases a credit score will use information from people the business has not paid on time to build up a view of financial standing. It would be sensible to address any major clients in this position to improve the overall rating.

Legal status

In addition, leasing can be a type of business funding that may be easier to access by an incorporated business rather than a partnership and especially a sole trader. While in the UK at least the tax position of both types of business format is broadly the same in terms of business reliefs, many leasing arrangements are not offered on the same terms to sole traders. This is largely because of an overlap between consumer credit legislation and equipment or vehicle leasing. This is especially noticeable in vehicle leasing where incorporation and a minimum turnover size may be required, or VAT registration.

WHO ARE THE SUPPLIERS OF LEASING AND OTHER ASSET FINANCE SERVICES?

Leasing and asset finance products are offered to the small business market from a wide range of sources. The structure of supply is similar to that of the invoice discounting and factoring market except that the number of alternative suppliers is probably even higher (Table 7.2).

Banks

All the main high street banks have leasing operations. The high street banks have an advantage in some respects, such as in the case of receivables finance, as they can filter firms that apply for debt funding in the first place towards leasing when needed. Even so, high street banks often find it difficult to articulate a positive advantage for debt versus lease arrangements when sold alongside each other, especially for small items. Many of the small customers of the high street banks are very small and not VAT registered. Also, in most cases, bank-sourced schemes do not have a maintenance or service plan from a supplier.

As a result high street banks tend to concentrate on larger leasing deals such as whole fleet funding or trains, ships and aircraft. Alternatively, banks offer a very niche product, often on an industry-specific basis, such as agricultural equipment or construction plant.

Independent providers

Investing the financial resources to set up and run a leasing business is an attractive proposition for many people, especially as it is a low-risk secured form of business

Table 7.2 *Leasing Equipment in the UK, 2013 – Asset Type*

		Selected Asset Types -				
	All Leasing	*Plant & Machinery*	*Commercial Vehicles*	*IT Equipment*	*Motor Vehicles*	*Other Business Equipment*
£ Million	21,712	4,473	5,189	1,542	6,753	1,926
12m % change	+4%	+4%	+9%	+14%	+1%	+1%

Source: Finance and Leasing Association Press Release, December 2013

finance funded in part in most countries by tax reliefs underwritten by government. Small independent firms can often secure debt funding from banks as well. Independent operators are very common in vehicle finance and specialised types of equipment where product knowledge is important. The independent firms often depend on a network of brokers to introduce business. In many cases, a business may well have contact with a broker who arranges the finance and may not be wholly sure of the ultimate source of the finance arrangement.

Larger corporates and product manufacturers

Manufacturers of capital goods and vehicles have a vested interest in ensuring customers can obtain funding for equipment purchases. As discussed in Chapter 4, a direct corporate loan market exists where manufacturers in particular use their own superior access to credit to source funding at cheaper rates than their end customers could get and then use this to fund their own suppliers. In the case of customers of many types of capital equipment as well, they are likely to acquire lease funding direct from a manufacturer (often tied into the sales process). These finance operations are funded off the balance sheet of the larger business. Especially in recent years, larger corporates in the UK, Europe and the USA for example have typically had a cheaper cost of funds than banks.

However, the main advantage for this group of suppliers is the link in with the initial sales process for the capital goods and the aftermarket (notably the maintenance contract and supply of spares). This integrated approach is very popular amongst small firms. Many small firms will look to purchase a new van or laptop and when in the showroom sort out the finance at the point of sale. This is nearly always a lease or HP arrangement. Similarly amongst smaller firms, especially sole traders, the supply of the leasing or HP arrangement can be from a retailer who offers this finance to personal customers as well.

CONCLUSION

Asset finance has the ability to provide a source of funding for both entrepreneurial and cash-flow purposes. The dual role is not common amongst external sources of small-firm finance when being used correctly. In addition, through the ability in the design of the product to maximise the use of tax allowances to the benefit of the customer, this form of funding widens access to a number of types of business in specialised situations that may otherwise have trouble with external funding. Finally, no other external finance product is so well integrated with the process for sale and aftermarket services. Many small business customers appreciate this integrated approach and the apparently less formalised credit risk process (although in reality this disguises a greater reliance on credit scoring rather than individual assessment).

BIBLIOGRAPHY

DELOOF, M., LAGAERT, I. and VERSCHUEREN, I. Leases and debt: complements or substitutes? Evidence from Belgian SMEs. *Journal of Small Business Management*, 45 (4), pp. 491–500, 2007.

KRAEMER-EIS, H. and LANG, F. The importance of leasing for SME financing, *EIF Working paper 2012/15*, Published online: www.eif.org/news_centre/research/eif_wp_2012_15_The%20importance%20of%20leasing%20for%20SME%20finance_August_2102.pdf (accessed 12 July 2014).

NEUBERGER, D. and RÄTHKE-DÖPPNER, S. Leasing by small enterprises, *Applied Financial Economics*, 23 (7), pp. 535–549, 2013.

DATA SOURCES

The UK Finance Leasing Association publishes regular statistics on the industry via a press release: www.financeleasingassociation.co.uk/index.php/media/press- releases/ (accessed 10 July 2014).

Chapter 8

Equity

Equity is initially created from the money first put into a business by its founders. This is the same for businesses of all sizes and types. However, equity and core capital play a different role in funding smaller private companies and unincorporated businesses than in larger corporates with publicly traded equity. Also, in practical terms, the definition of equity in smaller firms is wider and includes a number of related types of founder-based funding.

MORE ON THE ROLE OF EQUITY AND CORE CAPITAL IN SMALL FIRMS

For the purposes of this book, equity funding includes both the subscription to share capital in a company and less formal funding arrangements such as cash injections and director's loans and similar activities by sole traders and partnerships. Indeed, the terms 'equity', 'core capital' and 'retained profits' are treated here as largely meaning the same thing. After a firm has been set up, core capital is held as cash in the bank (deposits), combined with any surplus in the firm's balance sheet on net assets.

Once established, the core capital of a firm provides a vital on going role during the lifecycle of activity:

- At first, core capital is used to set up and develop a business, especially in a pre-revenue phase. Initially, this may mean the capital is needed to purchase or lease equipment, underpin bank loan applications or pay for premises and wages until orders are won and revenue is received.
- Once a business is up and running, retained profits can rebuild this capital base and so act as a buffer to support day-to-day cash-flow operations.
- In any subsequent periods of growth or contraction of a firm the adequacy of the equity base may also come under scrutiny again, requiring the initial investors to put in more capital or to add resources from new shareholders. The

discussion later in this chapter reviews sources of additional external equity that can be used if the retained profits of the business or the personal wealth of the owners and immediate family are insufficient to capitalise the business.

- Finally, the retained capital in a business is the ultimate determinant of the value of the venture should it be put up for sale. Most valuations will also include an assessment of the future prospects for revenue and profit. However, the bottom line is that the minimum value of a business is the scrap or resale value of any stock and assets plus the cash reserves after all debts have been settled.

The importance of the equity base of a business venture either in terms of share structure or less formal funding cannot be stressed enough. Indeed, firms in financial difficulties are often referred to as under-capitalised, implying they are seeking to operate on too little core capital and reliant too much on debt funding. Although this might appear to imply that equity is a critical form of cash-flow funding (it is the case that the free cash elements of core capital can help provide a trading buffer), in reality, equity is a key form of entrepreneurial funding needed to create or grow ventures. Firms in financial difficulty may have a cash-flow problem but in most cases this is generally regarded as being a consequence of poor entrepreneurial funding and management decisions either at the start of a venture or during implementation of a later period of business expansion.

Business longevity through sale and transfer

One aspect in which the distinction between equity and a more generic description of core capital remains useful concerns various aspects of the process of business transfer. The distinction also helps partly explain why companies tend to have longer business lifespans (the average age of the company stock in the UK is about eleven years, rather than about six years for all firms). Incorporated firms are also more likely to grow.

Formal equity is held as fully paid-up and issued shares in a company. In turn, this arrangement allows for more transparent arrangements to occur when selling a business and transferring ownership. In most small firms that are private companies with no external shareholders, all the equity will be owned by a few directors and the immediate family. All these shares can be sold to each other or third parties. The legal structure of the business can operate day-to-day despite these changes in ownership. New capital can be brought into the business through this sales process as well, or by issuing and selling more shares.

Partnership agreements seek to replicate some aspects of these transfer or sale arrangements. However, taking on a new partner or buying out an existing one technically requires one agreement to stop and a new one to start. A sole trader does not sell a business as such; they sell the assets and hopefully some allowance for goodwill. Any core capital left in a business run by a sole trader will be retained on sale. As a result, the average age of unincorporated businesses is lower than for companies. For many business owners, this makes little day-to-day difference but for some this turmoil hinders customer and supplier relationships and makes it difficult to raise equity funds for expansion. Indeed, some firms ultimately incorporate as a precursor to a period of investment for growth.

The difference between debt and equity – implications for profits and dividends

All commercial investors in a business hope to receive a financial return on the cash injected into a venture. For equity holders, this could be in the form of a dividend. In small private companies, the declaration of a dividend is often determined by tax regulation as owner directors have a degree of choice between declaring profits, with or without a dividend, or paying themselves more in terms of salary; they could also do neither of these things and instead build up reserves in the business. Even in profitable ventures, any regular dividend payments are largely optional without the scrutiny of publicly traded equity. The directors and private shareholders, for example, could all agree to take minimal salary payments, invest heavily and build up a business for sale. The ultimate financial return would be generated by the final sales price of the firm (taxed as a capital gain, often with some relief for investors in small companies), not a dividend stream (taxed as income and lacking many reliefs).

The key point though is that any dividend or drawings from the business are optional and reflect the success of the business in return for the capital invested. This is different from all other forms of finance that have to be repaid regardless of the current trading performance of the business. Also, if the firm ceases to trade, all or some of the capital invested in the firm could be lost as the shareholders have the lowest priority call on any funds left after debts are settled, whereas debt investors have a higher priority (especially secured lenders). Although this does not necessarily ensure debt holders get all the money back, they will always stand before equity holders in the queue.

Sole traders do not face the same choices as equity holders in companies. Sole traders' reserves as such would be regarded as profit by the tax authorities and cannot be set aside from income tax. The ability of a company to build up and hold reserves is another reason why they survive longer and grow more often than unincorporated firms.

SUCCESS FACTORS IN RAISING EXTERNAL CAPITAL

The initial founders of any enterprise could be wealthy enough in a personal capacity to have sufficient resources to inject all the necessary cash into a new venture.

This may well also include securing funds on less than strictly commercial terms from close family and friends, a not uncommon approach to sourcing initial funding. The business created from this personal or family investment could also generate enough cash through profitable trading to never need external equity funding. Many businesses, especially small firms, fall into this category and trade successfully using very little external funding at all (perhaps only a credit card, along with careful management of creditors and debtors). At least one-third of all small firms may fall into this category; they are resilient, stable firms in the business population but typically not fast growing.

However, both at start-up or particularly during subsequent periods of expansion, some business owners need to seek additional external investors into the business to increase the capital base. This is probably the case for between 5% and 10% of the business population at most at any time. While a minority in number, firms of this type are very important in terms of the business population as a whole as they are likely to include a high proportion of the fast-growing enterprises in the economy. What can business owners do in these circumstances to increase the likelihood of securing such external equity funding at an appropriate speed and cost? Also, how does this differ from seeking debt funding? (Table 8.1)

While the backgrounds and motivations of the broad spectrum of equity investors are wide and varied, if less commercial sources such as family and close friends

Table 8.1 *Use of Equity Funding for SMEs in the UK*

		By Employment Size-band			
Percentages	*All SMEs*	*0*	*1–9*	*10–49*	*50–249*
Using Loans or Equity in 2013 from:					
- *Directors*	5	3	9	11	11
- *Family or Friends*	5	5	7	3	2
*Sought from any commercial External Source 2011–2013**			<2	<4	<6

* As a percentage of the total SME population, use of true external equity is exceptionally rare. This estimate is based on the Small Business Survey 2012 data which cites the incidence of 2% of SME employers seeking finance. However, only 24% of the population sought finance that year. The 2004 survey of SME Finance cited a figure of 3% over the period 2002–2004

Sources:

(1) SME Finance Monitor, Q42013 Report, tables page 47

(2) Dept. for Business Innovation and Skills, Small Business Survey 2012: SME Employers, April 2013, URN BIS/P24, Tables 7.2 and 7.5.

(3) S. Fraser, Finance for Small and Medium-sized Enterprises: A Report on the 2004 UK Survey of SME Finances, University of Warwick, 2005, pages 114–115.

(4) Authors estimates – see *

are excluded, any true external commercial investor is essentially seeking favourable answers for three questions:

- How high is the likelihood of success for this venture run by this team of owners and key staff?
- How much will it cost to buy into this potential income stream compared with the future reward?
- What is the exit route from this investment in the future?

These are linked considerations and can be summarised as establishing an investor's risk-reward 'appetite'. A potential investor may well recognise the business has a high chance of success but so do many others. As a result, the price of entry is high and the returns are modest. A much better outcome for the investor is to identify a business idea or development opportunity that no other investors have found with a lower entry price, so the projected returns on the deal are much higher. Alternatively, some investors will seek investments where the likelihood of success at all may be lower, securing a low entry cost, yet is still attractive as the potential upside return if all goes well is very high. For serial investors, even when they buy into a company this may be conditional on the business providing them with a way to sell up over a fixed term (e.g. a trade sale in five years). In other cases, an investor may look for a lower but stable return and not be bothered about an exit opportunity (at least to start with).

Striking a balance between these two factors creates a tension in all investment decisions regardless of the type or size of investor. Similar considerations also cover a wide range of transaction types ranging from a small cash injection to support the expansion of an established business to full-scale management buy-out and buy-in deals. These risk-reward choices are very personal to investors, especially smaller investors.

Understanding and successfully addressing this source of potential friction should assist business owners seeking to raise external equity funds. Successful businesses seeking external equity need to persuade the investor that they match their risk-reward profile. For example:

- A single external investor in a business – sometimes referred to as a business angel – may be looking for more involvement in the day-to-day management of a firm, or offer mentor support. This, in turn, may get reflected in the commercial decisions and agreed investment price.
- Groups of shareholders or professionally run portfolio investors are normally keener on security and certainty of future revenue. Also, even at the point of investment, these investors may well have an eye on the ultimate exit route for selling the investment for a higher price at a later date.

Moreover, it is useful to consider how these questions about the likelihood of success and the price of the investment impact upon the decision process for a truly commercial equity investor and to see how this varies from that of a debt investor such as a bank manager. In a number of ways, similarities can be seen between the appraisal process from a debt and equity investment point of view:

- Equity investors will undertake a process of due diligence to consider all the legal aspects of any potential investment. The forensic examination of management accounts, legal titles and agreements, patents and personal background of the directors is commonplace for corporate-type transactions. For smaller equity arrangements or new partnerships, a less formal number of enquiries will be made as well. These checks are not too dissimilar to those made by a bank's credit assessment. A bank manager has some advantage in that the firm and its directors could have been customers for many years and can look at the transaction history to help inform a view. Potential equity investors will almost certainly ask directors to disclose this sort of information as well.
- A key requirement for a bank assessment is to identity a source of repayment of any new debt facility that has a very high probability of being received. A signed contract with a reputable third party is best but in other situations a track record of the business in doing this before, and security or personal guarantees help reduce the uncertainty. Depending on the stage of the equity investment, similar questions are asked as well. Only a proportion of equity investors will have a risk-reward appetite to seed fund true pre-revenue situations, so existing and new revenue streams are also a key part of the decision to invest in most cases.

However, despite the similarities, equity investors are still taking into account different risk-reward issues from a loan appraisal; these also need to be addressed successfully by businesses seeking external funds. Despite all the due diligence and checking, equity investors know they must be entering into a riskier investment than a debt provider. Investors will constantly have in the back of their mind a question: 'If this is such a secure investment, why don't the business owners just borrow the money and not dilute their future profits?' Firms looking for external equity support need to successfully answer this for the investor. The reasons used to justify equity not debt in such circumstances will normally include a mixture of reasons such as:

- Balance sheet issues – the need for more core capital in the business as the firm is under-capitalised and cannot support any new debt. New capital may be needed to secure more debt to fully fund expansion plans.
- Risk – the proposal is a high-growth project that necessarily has a high level of risk associated with it. As such the likelihood of success for the project is

too low to attract debt funding given its fixed upper limit of return (capital repayment plus interest).

- Personal – the businesses will benefit from an equity investor joining the management team or becoming a partner (or in some way offering mentoring support).

All these reasons tend to place the equity investor in a strong negotiating position at the start of discussions with a firm seeking investment. The challenge for the existing owners of a business is the need to get the right deal for them and the investor. What is sometimes not fully appreciated is that how well the current owners negotiate is part of the assessment process by investors as well.

The issue of why equity is needed, in turn, highlights again the dilemma between the likelihood of success in a venture and the price of investing in the business to gain access to the profits. Consequently, it is generally regarded that in equity deals discussion and negotiation are often just as intense on the price or terms of the deal as much as the basic assessment of project viability. In debt negotiations, the emphasis is mainly on the decision to lend with price being a secondary issue, especially in the small business marketplace.

- An equity investor wants to pay the lowest possible price for buying into a business to minimise losses if the business fails but also to maximise the return on the full upside potential of the investment.
- A debt provider such as a bank only wants the money back with interest and a degree of profit from each applicant. A debt provider has little or no financial interest in how successful one venture will be compared with another once the debt repayment has been assured. They have no stake in any upside. An equity investor, on the other hand, wants to identify an investment with the most upside potential as they will benefit from this being attained. This is particularly the case for an investor with a portfolio of high-risk assets where the losses of the majority of projects can be offset by the maximum upside being achieved by one or two successful ventures elsewhere.

How negotiations are conducted illustrates another more generic issue for firms seeking new equity investors or partners. These decisions often depend very much on interpersonal relationships, especially if the investor will be active in the business in any way. People have to work with each other. Even the best-prepared proposals for investment can fail if the various people involved do not get on. In extreme cases, some individual equity investors suggest they make a decision in principle on whether they could work with a management team within a few minutes of a first meeting, even before they look at the idea or any paperwork. Such a high involvement in social skills and personal relationships is now very unlikely to be a major consideration in applying for a bank loan or other forms of debt or rental agreements. Debt investment, even if arranged by a bank relationship manager, is essentially an arm's length financial transaction.

SOURCES OF NEW EXTERNAL EQUITY FOR UK SMES

The range of equity sources for small firms is extremely broad with an equally complex spread of investor objectives. Even with non-commercial investors excluded from this review, notably family and friends, the observation holds true (Table 8.2).

However, the different groups of equity investors all have varying levels of risk tolerance and expected returns on the funds committed. These range from replacement partners – who are effectively buying into an established business and want a salary as much as dividends – to private equity funds seeking significant returns for unproven ventures and may be looking for the sale of the investment within five to seven years. The amount of equity each investor group can offer a single venture also follows a similar scale with some investors supporting different stages of business growth, one after another. This often leads to a discussion of a 'funding escalator', which is examined in more detail in a later chapter.

Replacement business partners

This is an often overlooked but very common form of equity investment for small firms. Most businesses start with a sole owner or a group of owners. Over time, as a business survives and grows it is likely that where a partnership exists one or more of them will seek to withdraw from the firm for a variety of reasons. One

Table 8.2 *Indicators of SME Equity Investment Activity in the UK, 2012–13*

Equity Source	*£m New Funds, 2012–13*	*No. of Deals/Companies*
Business Angel funding	£76	262
Venture Capital	£5,764	820
*EIS – new applications **	£1,017	1498
*VCT – new funds raised **	£370	–
Crowd-funded Equity	£30	–
British Business Bank	£150	250
Business Growth Fund	£200	200

* Note UK tax relief schemes. EIS is the Enterprise Investment Scheme and VCT covers a range of Venture Capital Trust schemes

Sources:
(1) British Business Angel Survey, 2012/13
(2) British Venture Capital Association Investment Activity Report, 2012
(3) HMRC Statistics
(4) NESTA, The Rise of Alternative Finance, 2013
(5) British Business Bank, Strategy Update, 2014
(6) Business Growth Fund Review, 2013
(7) Company websites and author estimates

partner could seek to retire, or raise funds for another business venture. Also, it could be as simple as the founder partners just having an argument and falling out and are no longer willing to work together for a common purpose. Or, of course, a partner could die and their interest will become part of their estate.

In circumstances such as this the other members of the partnership – which could be a small private company or an unincorporated business – have a choice. Like a sole trader wanting to withdraw from a firm, they could offer the business for sale and break the partnership up. Alternatively, the remaining partners could put more cash into the business and buy out the shareholding. This way the business could continue and the remaining partners would have bought the rights to a greater share of the profits of the venture going forward. A third option is a new partner could be sought to buy in to the firm, effectively purchasing the share of the business directly from the partner seeking to retire.

These types of replacement investment affect many thousands of firms a year, although it is not often acknowledged in reviews of the equity market. In part, this is understandable as the new investor is probably just replacing an existing one on a like-for-like basis. The capital base of the firm is not being increased as such. Indeed, as the new investor is buying into a going concern, he or she is not taking the same risks as the founder investors did. Even so, this is still a form of entrepreneurial finance. Without the new investor, the business would be very unlikely to survive unless the other shareholders could increase the stake.

Little is really known about the scale and operation of this type of equity investment. New partners are often sought by word of mouth, or with the help of the firm's accountant. How these investment opportunities are valued is also difficult to monitor. However, more formal arrangements and networks tend to operate in some business sectors, notably professional services. It is most evident and much more organised amongst GPs and dentists but similar less formal arrangements take place across all sectors and business types.

High net worth individuals (business angels)

Another group of private and personal equity investors are business angels. These are high net worth individuals seeking investment opportunities for their wealth. Angel investors may operate on a solo basis or in a group via a syndicate (sometimes with the help of a coordinator such as an accountant or investment adviser).

Business angels have a wide range of personal objectives. Some are wealthy people seeking an attractive home for surplus cash. In other cases, professional angel investors are looking for a succession of businesses to support. Quite frequently, solo investors are looking for an opportunity to become involved in the day-to-day affairs of the venture through a role on the board. Stereotypically, these are often senior executives or successful business owners seeking an interest after retirement from their first career. Alternatively, and perhaps more typically in recent years, they are people seeking to reinvest a portion of the proceeds from a successful exit of a previous business venture.

A similar range of motives and means of operation are in place for syndicate investors. In some cases, this may be little more than a small group of friends who all have some surplus cash to invest. In other cases, it could be a very large group of investors operating on a semi-professional basis with technical support. A common thread though is that syndicate investors are obviously seeking to spread risk more than a solo investor, suggesting more of a preference for investment income than direct personal involvement in the business (which would be difficult via a group investment approach anyway).

In the case of solo investors especially, business angels can look very similar to finding a new replacement partner. However, significant differences are apparent between the two groups.

- Business angels when they seek management involvement are looking for a mentoring role and a seat on the board, very rarely full-time day-to-day employment.
- Also, business angels will be linking investment with a recognisable call for new funds to grow and develop a business. A replacement partner will typically be seeking to replace the founder capital of a current owner who is looking to withdraw.
- Moreover, while national schemes and rules vary, in most OECD countries angel investors have the opportunity to get significant tax relief on the investment and this is a key attraction. Normally these tax-based schemes have limits on the scale of investment that can be made in any one business and the degree of management involvement allowed as well. In contrast, a replacement owner will typically have to buy a large part of the business and not get such tax relief. However, in some cases angel investors do ignore tax reliefs as well and would rather have the freedom to invest in business ventures without the need to do this in a tax-efficient way.

Corporate investments (corporate venturing)

Direct investment by one business in another is another source of equity for expanding firms. This is typically a minority stake by one larger firm in an unquoted business and is often called corporate venturing. The motives for making such an investment are rarely just based on immediate financial return. Rather, investment may be offered willingly by one business, or actively sought by the other, as a way to tie the two firms closer together without a full takeover. It could be that the minority shareholding is a way for a larger corporate to nurture and monitor the development of a new technology or market with a view to ultimately offering to buy the business outright. Alternatively, a minority shareholding may be taken to fund investment in a product or service that is a key input to the larger firm's operations. As with investments by high net worth individuals, these shareholdings often lead to formal recognition of the arrangement via board representation.

Equity funds

Dedicated funds provide a professional source of equity finance. These funds may only assist a small percentage of larger SMEs a year in each national market but these firms normally have significant growth prospects both in terms of revenue and employment. As a result, the investment from these funds is a key element of the finance landscape and the business environment. All these funds are professionally managed and offer significant equity investments in firms with growth prospects over a five–seven-year period (after which the firms will typically be looking for an exit either to a quoted market or direct placement with a long-term investor). Equity investments of this type all have the capability to transform an individual business in scale and growth trajectory.

Equity funds fall into three main groups broadly distinguished by the source of funding. They all operate in the same way by seeking out and appraising investment opportunities placed in front of them. However, the funding source may influence the types of firm supported or the nature of the investment made.

Publicly backed

A vibrant and well-funded private equity industry is recognised by most national governments as a key national asset for economic development. As a result, many countries have a long history of intervention to create and promote funds where supply is seen as inadequate. The form of public support can either be through direct funding from tax revenues or granting various forms of tax relief on private subscriptions to equity funds.

Typically, public involvement in the creation and funding of these equity funds also has an influence on subsequent activities. In the case of funds directly capitalised by the taxpayer, the money may be targeted at certain higher-risk areas of business activity but with strategic national importance (such as high-tech or medical research). Alternatively, the recipient groups could be limited to a range of under-represented groups in enterprise activity such as women-owned firms or those run by ex-armed forces. More commonly, investments could be linked to a single regional market to support local economic development.

The alternative way for public intervention – taxpayer supported subscription funds – normally have more freedom of operation on investments. Rather, while it is normal to have some limitation on the size of individual investments and that of the recipient company, regional, special interest or sector limitations are not common. It may be though that subscription-backed funds with public support have a time limitation on when onward initial investments can be made to ensure the accumulated funds are invested rather than left to sit unused.

Equity funds capitalised with public funds still all have as their ultimate objective an exit from the individual profitable investments to, as a minimum, make the work self-funding. Profits made will offset losses on other investments and the net gain is normally recycled. However, given the nature of some of the markets selected, these tend to be longer-term very patient funds. Indeed, in some cases, the public funds impose a limit on the upside financial return they receive in an order to tempt the private sector to come in and take over the investments as they mature. Publicly supported subscription funds tend to have much more freedom to return funds to initial investors after a period of time, allowing the net profits from the funds to be distributed.

Private equity

Privately capitalised equity funds are resourced from investments made by longer-term investors such as pension funds or insurance companies and seek to generate a fully commercial return. Again, as in the case of the public funds, these are substantial and professionally managed activities and a key part of the national financial infrastructure. The fund managers seek out or consider investment offers to secure growth and a profitable investment over a three–seven-year period. The equity will then be sold, normally to another private equity firm, a management buy-out or a junior market listing. It could also be – less commonly – sold to a long-term investor such as a pension fund. In all cases, the profits made by the private equity firm will be returned to the fund for investment again (Table 8.3).

While private equity funds will of course have losses from failed ventures, it is more likely the private funds will be hit by lower financial returns than expected than outright loss. Directly capitalised public funds may well look at higher-risk

Table 8.3 *BVCA member Investment Activity in the UK, 2012*

	£m New Funds	*No. Companies*	*£m Avg. Deal Size*
Early Stage	£343	413	£0.83
Core Capital	£1,471	296	£4.97
Replacement Capital	£1,286	44	£29.23
MBO/MBI	£2,677	100	£26.77
Other Late Stage	£143	25	£5.72
Total	£5,766	820	£7.03

Source: British Venture Capital Association Investment Activity Report, 2012

investments. Private equity more often considers second and third waves of equity investment. Indeed, private equity funds especially have a number of sub-markets of activity with different levels of risk and reward:

- Some funds specialise in start-up and early stage investments that may have a higher failure rate (surviving investments for these types of funds tend to have very substantial upside investment return to offset these losses).
- In volume terms, the bulk of funds are directed at established business growth opportunities where losses may be lower and investment returns are more widely spread through a portfolio.
- Private equity funds will support management buy-in and buy-out operations, where firms with potential are taken over by a new team of directors with equity backing. In a buy-in scenario, the existing owners sell to a new management team. In a management buy-out, the existing managers buy the firm from the current owners. All need equity support to achieve the ownership change.

Bespoke funds

Equity funds normally subscribe to new shares in companies with growth potential to generate an investment return. However, more bespoke funds also operate that may well provide a mixture of debt and equity or linked products. The use of debt and equity in this way looks like the operation of a traditional merchant bank. Indeed, the reasons for this type of investment is that the firm supported may well be too small to support large-scale equity investment at this stage and even after a period of substantial growth are unlikely to be attractive to long-term investors, which is the exit strategy of private equity. Hence, bespoke funds have emerged to support these even smaller firms with growth potential.

Again, funding of these bespoke activities is from a mixture of public and private sources. Quite often, banks will fund these operations as they provide a way for customers to obtain some equity support alongside existing banking arrangements. The key requirement is longer-term patient funding rather than the three–seven-year lifecycle for a private equity fund. Investments are more likely to be of 15–20-year duration.

Public equity markets, such as a formal stock exchange, have little direct engagement with small-business funding. Even rapidly growing firms supported by private equity are unlikely to be offered to a public market as a next stage of funding. More likely is that a bespoke fund would consider offering very long-term investments to more lightly regulated unlisted security markets as one possible exit route. However, these are very few in number and even junior stock market listings are regarded as out of scope of this review.

CONCLUSION

The ability of owners to access external equity funding is a key element in small firms' funding, especially for entrepreneurial businesses seeking to grow. The equity needed could be still small in scale, particularly when a partnership or a block of shares held by a single director comes up for sale. In other cases, external equity funding can be large in scale and transformational to businesses' growth prospects.

Equity investors come in many shapes and sizes and work at all stages of a business in conjunction with other sources of external finance. Often, the willingness or ability of people to inject equity into a business venture reflects the risk-reward objectives of the investor set against the type of funding required by the business. This highlights the need to look at how external finance can flex and change over the course of a business lifecycle.

BIBLIOGRAPHY

BVCA, *Guide to Private Equity*, Published online, 2012: www.bvca.co.uk/Portals/0/library/Files/Website%20files/2012_0001_guide_to_private_equity.pdf (accessed 12 July 2014).

BVCA, *The Missing Piece: How corporate venture capital can transform UK finance and funding*, Published online 2013: www.bvca.co.uk/Portals/0/library/documents/BVCA%20The%20Missing%20Piece.pdf (accessed 12 July 2014).

BUSINESS GROWTH FUND *Branching Out: How Capital Growth Can Fund Success, Review 2012/3*, Published online, 2013: www.businessgrowthfund.co.uk/wp-content/uploads/2013/07/Review-2013.pdf (accessed 12 July 2014).

BUSINESS GROWTH FUND *Review 2013/4*, Published online, 2014: www.businessgrowthfund.co.uk/wp-content/uploads/2014/06/BGF-REVIEW-2014-.pdf (accessed 12 July 2014).

GILLIGAN, J. and WRIGHT, M. *Private Equity Demystified: An Explanatory Guide*, London, ICAEW, 2nd Ed., 2010.

MASON, C., HARRISON, R.T. and GREAT BRITAIN, DEPARTMENT FOR BUSINESS, INNOVATION AND SKILLS *Annual Report on the Business Angel Market in the UK, 2008/9 (BIS research paper)*, London, BIS (URN 10/994), 2010.

MASON, C., HARRISON, R.T. and GREAT BRITAIN, DEPARTMENT FOR BUSINESS, INNOVATION AND SKILLS *Annual Report on the Business Angel Market in the UK, 2009/10 (BIS research paper)*, London, BIS (URN 11/P116), 2011.

NESTA and BVCA *From Funding Gaps to Thin Markets: UK Government Support for Early Stage Venture Capital*, London, NESTA, 2009.

OECD *Financing High-Growth Firms: The Role of Angel Investors*, Brussels, OECD Publishing, 2011.

ROD BALL, R., BURROWS, A., HOWORTH, C.A., KLOECKNER, O., SCHOLES, L., WESTHEAD, P. and WRIGHT, M. *Private Equity in Family Firms: A Report on Private Equity Investments in Family Firms Across Europe,* Nottingham University: The Centre for Management Buy-out Research, 2008.

SQW CONSULTING *The Supply of Equity Finance to SMEs: Revisiting the Equity Gap (BIS research paper),* London, BIS (URN 09/1573), 2009.

UKBBAA and DELOITTE *Taking the Pulse of the Angel Market,* Published online, 2013: www.ukbusinessangelsassociation.org.uk/sites/default/files/media/files/taking_pulse_of_the_angel_market_02_07_2013_0.pdf (accessed 12 July 2014).

WILTBANK, R.E. *Siding with the Angels: Business Angel Investing – Promising Outcomes and Effective Strategies,* London, NESTA, 2009.

DATA SOURCES

The BVCA publishes regular and extensive data on UK and European investment trends and returns. www.bvca.co.uk/ResearchPublications/IndustryStatistics.aspx (accessed 10 July 2014).

Data on Management Buyouts related equity deals is also collected by the Centre for Management Buyout Research: wwwf.imperial.ac.uk/business-school/research/the-centre-for-management-buy-out-research/uk-equity/ (accessed 10 July 2014).

A number of the sources quoted in the bibliography are a combination of research articles and annual review data.

Part III

A longer-term view

Chapter 9

The use of external finance over time: escalators and rollercoasters

In previous chapters of this study covering aspects of small-business finance, the two broad types of funding have been considered – cash-flow and entrepreneurial funding – and a number of specific lines of funding have been reviewed in detail. However, in this chapter the objective is to look at these different types of funding together and see how firms use them over time. This will provide a firm-level case study to link together the various aspects of external finance under consideration.

Initially, this chapter discusses the funding escalator, a very useful starting point often used in studies of small-firm finance. However, more emphasis is given to a funding rollercoaster as well; this is an extension of the escalator idea to represent more accurately the funding lifecycle. Finally, some of the key external influences on the funding landscape such as the business cycle are looked at in more detail.

THE FUNDING ESCALATOR

One of the most commonly used ways of presenting a time-based approach to external funding for small firms is the funding escalator. In the escalator, normally shown in a visual format, a firm begins at the bottom step and then moves up over time using different types of funding. Access to different levels of funding is closely associated with growth. At the top step, the business has grown into a substantial enterprise and is being funded through sophisticated equity activities and, in some versions, publically traded markets (Figure 9.1).

The funding escalator is a very useful visualisation of the time-based approach to external sources of business funding. It is notably helpful in concentrating attention on each upward step and the problems faced by firms in making this move forward. This is particularly the case for public policy where a lot of attention is paid to potential market gaps and failures at each step in the process.

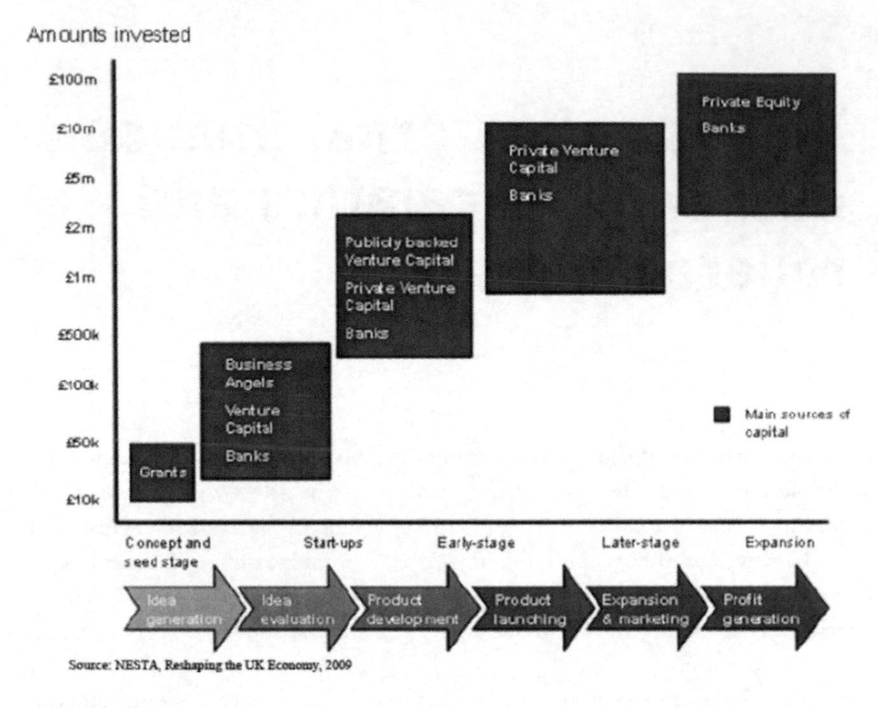

Figure 9.1
Funding Escalator

However, the escalator approach does have some important limitations:

- In reality of course not all firms make a successful journey from the bottom to the top of the escalator and little consideration is made of the circumstances why this happens.
- The presentation of the rising steps to indicate growth only tends to be truly applicable to a small number of firms. Most businesses do not grow rapidly, or indeed year on year. The use of external finance is more widespread in the business population than just rapid business growth (the group of firms for which the analysis was mainly developed).
- External funding is more often used at various phases of a business life but this is rarely a continuous activity. In slacker periods, a firm may be wholly funded from retained profits and careful cash-flow management.

THE FUNDING ROLLERCOASTER

An extension of the visual presentation of the time-based view of business funding from the escalator is the funding rollercoaster. This develops the escalator model to address the issues discussed above. In particular, the rollercoaster presented in

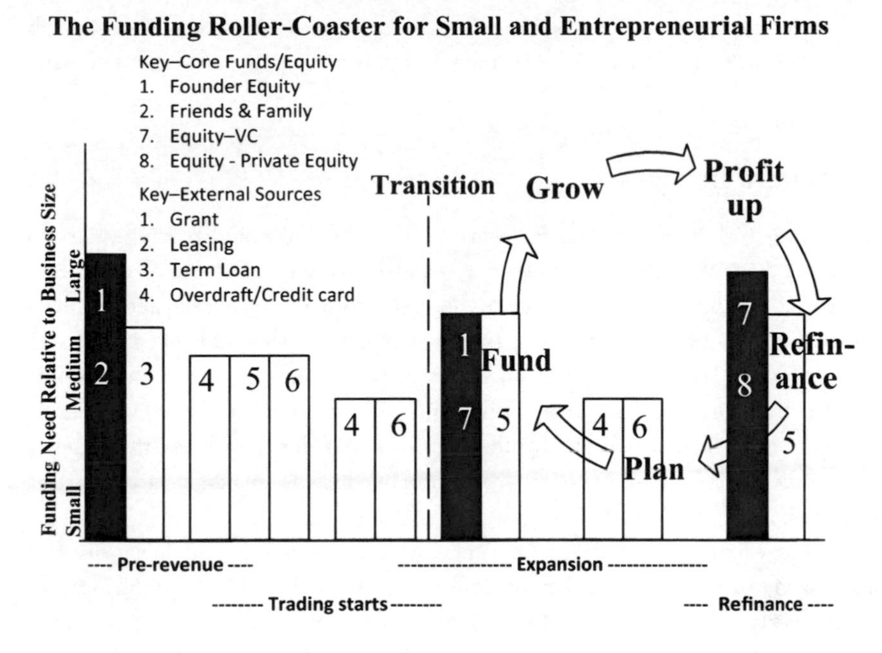

Figure 9.2
The Funding Rollercoaster graph

this chapter illustrates 'waves' of activity but without the steps to indicate growth. As a result, the rollercoaster can apply just as well to fairly short-lived enterprises that never seek to grow very much (Figure 9.2).

Looking at the rollercoaster in more detail highlights a number of phases of funding.

Pre-start/pre-revenue

In this stage the emphasis is mainly on entrepreneurial funding from the personal capital injected into the business by the founder and family and friends, as well as non-commercial sources such as grants or soft government-backed loans. It is very rare for a pre-revenue start-up to secure any form of commercial debt funding without a proven income source for repayment (equipment leasing may be possible). However, a small number of businesses with substantial long-term investment potential may successfully obtain pre-revenue equity investment.

The initial trading phase

This phase may be reached very quickly as few firms want to stay in a pre-revenue phase for very long. Once a firm begins to record a trading income the possibility of using commercial sources of external cash-flow finance increase – probably a bank overdraft at first and maybe a credit card. At the same time, a trading business will be looking to give and receive trade credit and manage cash-flow on a daily basis.

The transition phase

Many firms that have survived from pre-revenue to successful trading often go through a transition phase after about 18 months to two years into business life. The exact timing will vary of course depending on the circumstances of each business. In this phase, the business owner may have to extend capacity but also repay informal loans from family and friends used to set up. This withdrawal of initial entrepreneurial resources is often linked to using a structured bank loan, leasing or asset finance product for the first time in order to stabilise the finances (unless the business is so profitable early on and this source can be used for this purpose).

For many firms, the transition phase may well be as far as they go in a particular business venture. A successful transition consolidates the day-to-day finances to create a fairly stable business platform. Some firms cannot make the transition with enterprise closure rates reaching a peak at this time. The initial personal enthusiasm people had to set up a firm may have faded when faced with the day-to-day reality of running a business. A large number of owners just close a business and go back into paid employment. Alternatively, some owners cannot make the transition because they are unable to find the external funding. The business may not be profitable enough to support commercial external finance, or the owners are unable to present the business case well enough.

Even amongst surviving firms, in many cases the business has started and survived and got its trading activities on an even keel. However, the business owner has no desire to go further. The owner can draw an income from the business and the firm can manage on its current finance structure with careful cash-flow management and its core equity base as a buffer.

However, this is not the case for all small firms. Some have the ambition to go further. As discussed in Chapter 2, between 20% and 30% of smaller businesses seek external finance a year. As a result, further more optional phases can be identified.

Expansion phase(s)

If the businesses owners seek to grow to a scale that can be funded from within the business, they require additional entrepreneurial sources of funding to get growth off the ground. At first, this may involve further injections of personal equity alongside bank loans and commercial mortgages. However, successful firms often go through several phases of expansion. Subsequent waves may well need use of more transformational sources of funding, notably new external equity of various types. In expansion phases, cash-flow-based funding is still used as well but additional external funding is set up and taken on.

Replacement phase(s)

Between expansion phases, it is common for the business owners to look to consolidate the business operations, as well as replace and update equipment and ensure the business finances are streamlined as much as possible. In the replacement waves, external funding needs will move back towards using more cash-flow-based sources of funding.

Closure phase

All firms eventually go through a closure phase. For some, it may occur soon after a brief period of trading that does not go well. For others, it could be decades later after many years of growth and profitable activity. Even at closure, most firms do not fail or default on debts. Rather, they are sold in a variety of ways to new owners or the assets are realised and debts are paid. However, for a minority of businesses the closure phase can involve a range of sources of finance. Equity funds may well provide an exit route for a minority of business owners, using this source of funding to sell the business as a going concern to a new management team and allow them to withdraw the capital.

OTHER ENVIRONMENTAL ISSUES

When looking at a time-based view of external finance, the concept of the funding rollercoaster provides a very useful way to map out developments over time. However, the guidance provided by the phases of the rollercoaster for the behaviour of individual small firms at any point in time still has limitations.

Any model of behaviour such as the rollercoaster – or indeed the escalator – can only really cover what is likely to be the behaviour of a 'typical' or 'average' small firm during a period of 'normal' economic activity. It is obvious that all small businesses are actually different, notably because the people that run them are different themselves in so many ways. These variations may be just as much about personal and social circumstances rather than business aspirations alone. This is a key contrast with the activities of larger firms, where operational and accountancy guidelines and frameworks ensure firms operate in fairly standard ways. Consequently, further things need to be taken into account to illustrate correctly how the external funding environment operates for small firms over time.

Two major additional environmental factors require further comment.

The economic cycle both at a national and local level

Even during a 'typical' economic cycle, opportunities will vary to a degree during an upswing and a subsequent downswing. Business owners can sensibly alter the timing and scale of their ambition to reflect this pattern. It can also influence external funding sources used as well as the timing. For example, in an upswing a lot of new firms may enter the core market of an established small firm, so the owners may decide to delay debt-based expansion plans and redirect cash-flow resources to improving service in core activities by taking on more staff. The owners may decide that investing in customer services may be the best way to meet the competitive threat from new entrants. Or, in a downswing in economic activity, business owners may be more willing to introduce external equity to part fund a new venture as a way of sharing risk more than funding entirely from personal assets or even bank debt.

The personal lifecycle of the business owners

While it is an obvious point, it is rarely mentioned that businesses are run by people. Business owners do not leave personal circumstances at the office door as they start work every day. In smaller firms, this can be a key environmental factor in a number of business decisions, including finance. It has already been noted that not all firms have growth ambitions and, once established, firms may well seek to just stay in a safe steady state. More generally, the personal circumstances of different owners can impact on business funding choices. For example, a business owner with a young family may well decide to delay expansion plans to prioritise family life. Or, they may decide to favour buying a bigger house with personal wealth rather than increasing the capital base of a business. Later on, of course, succession planning and retirement issues can also influence attitude towards sourcing new development plans through equity, especially bringing new investors into the business.

Both factors – economic and personal – overlay the funding rollercoaster discussed earlier. As a result, the number of possible permutations becomes endless and unique to a firm. In this way, while it is possible to talk about average behaviour of a firm in relation to its external funding, in reality of course this covers a very wide range of variation. All these issues need to be looked at to truly unravel the funding pattern of a single firm. Also, care is required to assume one firm can and should follow the funding path of another successful business as this may not be transferable when other environmental conditions vary.

The phases of the business finance rollercoaster and other environmental factors are illustrated by a case study to accompany this chapter. The framework used to present the information is also a useful approach for a student of small-business finance to examine the funding pattern of any business.

CASE STUDY – MIDLANDS MOTOR COMPONENTS LTD.

Outline description

Midlands Motor Components Ltd (MMC) was set up in 2000 by three ex-foremen and an accountant who had all worked in the car component sector for years. The original manufacturing facility employed six other people at start-up (although the business took a few months to get off the ground when the owner–directors worked on the idea and purchased plant etc.). The initial production plant used one complete plastic injection moulding kit to supply car fascia components to one UK car plant. The start-up cost was £100,000 to commence production. The original directors raised £20,000 each from savings and equity release on houses they owned (or in one case, owned by a family member who loaned the money to the director to invest). In addition, a three-year contract with a national car producer allowed them to lease the specialised equipment and PCs to fund the production line; a total of £20,000 of new equipment was rented via a finance lease costing £350 a month over three years (with an option to purchase at the end). The directors' cash funding was used, in part, to fund the upfront lease payments on the production site, staff training and the first set of injection moulds to meet the agreed specification in the three-year contract. Turnover in year one was about £120,000 and after expenses and lease costs the firm just about broke even (although all the directors did draw a salary).

MMC is still trading in 2012/13 and has grown to about 100 staff with a full-year turnover of £5 million. However, this growth has not been linear but has gone through a number of phases.

- A period of rapid growth occurred from 2000 to 2004. The firm had one major contract, good terms of trade for payment and a strong buffer of founder capital.
- Growth stopped between 2004 and 2006. Indeed, sales actually fell for a few months in 2005 and some staff had to be laid off. The original contract with one car plant was not renewed. The business was obliged to look for smaller, less regular contracts with new suppliers. As a result, based on a good trading history, the firm sought an increased overdraft limit to ease worries over debtor payments. Some of the original equipment was getting worn out and inefficient, while rising oil prices were becoming an issue, especially as raw material suppliers demanded quicker payment. The firm continued to replace and upgrade equipment on an ad hoc basis via lease finance.
- A period of rapid growth returned again between 2006 and 2008. This was linked to a new relationship with a car manufacturer building a brand new line and offered them a five-year contract. The contract required the development of a dedicated and up-to-date production plant and so needed substantial investment. This was funded in part by additional equity from the

directors and a commercial mortgage on new premises (the mortgage had a fixed interest rate till 2011 but the repayments were easily funded from the new income generated).

- From 2008 to 2010, the international financial crisis and rising energy prices raised a concern for the company, especially as the 2006 contract with one customer was due to end in 2011. However, the 2006 contract was renegotiated with the car manufacturer helping the firm secure finance on good terms (otherwise the fixed rate on the mortgage would have ended in 2011, threatening a cash-flow issue). Growth was modest but employment levels were held steady. Even so, 2011 still proved to be a difficult year as one of the original directors retired and wanted to withdraw from the business. He held 25% of the shares, valued at just over £1 million (from an original investment of £20,000 plus some additional funds totalling £70,000 over 12 years).
- By 2013, MMC had got over the problem, aided by economic recovery and strong orders for car components. A new shareholder was found, although they do not have a day-to-day role in the business. The three original directors bought out the retiring director's shareholdings for £1 million. The incoming director purchased newly issued shares in MMC valued at £1.3 million for a 25% share in the re-capitalised business. This new capital has been held in reserve as the business negotiates new work to expand further.

Discussion

MMC is a successful company and typical of many small firms in the UK. The narrative history outlined can be used to populate a funding grid to consider in more detail cash-flow and entrepreneurial funding activities over its business lifespan (Table 9.1).

The grid, along with the narrative, reinforces the key points of the funding rollercoaster discussed earlier in this chapter.

- Growth is not linear and at times the business stops expanding.
- Cash-flow funding has been a requirement of the business throughout, although the means of providing this funding have changed at times.
- Entrepreneurial funding has been required at distinct times in MMC's business lifespan, especially in 2000, 2006 and 2012. At other times, this type of funding has been more modest.
- The business has been impacted by both the economic cycle and the personal decision of a director to retire and withdraw his investment, forcing the other directors to act.

Table 9.1 *MMC Funding Trends, 2000–2013*

Phase	*Cash-flow funds*	*Entrepreneurial funds*	*Activity*
Pre-revenue	Credit card – personal not business at first	Founder capital, family and friends cash	Equipment lease set up, negotiate initial contract, find and rent premises, train staff
Initial Trading	Bank overdraft,	Leasing	Production starts
Transition	Bank overdraft limit increased	Leasing	Replacement of original equipment, move to multiple contracts
Expansion	Bank overdraft, factoring	Commercial mortgage, new founder equity	Large expansion of facilities, site purchased, factoring added to ease cash flow
Replacement/ Refinance	Bank overdraft, factoring	New director brings in cash to buy out founder. Additional founder equity. Refinance of mortgage	New board add to capital base as well as replace retiring director. Funds used to reduce borrowing where possible. Mortgage refinanced on good terms (support from customer with bank)
Expansion	Bank overdraft, factoring	Leasing – being considered for equipment but business cash positive with funds on deposit	Bidding for new contract 2013 – funds available to tool up for orders and extend site

BIBLIOGRAPHY

GREAT BRITAIN, DEPARTMENT FOR BUSINESS, INNOVATION AND SKILLS *SME Access to External Finance (BIS Economics paper 16)*, London, BIS (URN 12/539), 2012.

COAD, A., FRANKISH, J., ROBERTS, R.G. and STOREY, D.J. Growth paths and survival chances: an application of Gambler's Ruin theory, *Journal of Business Venturing*, 28 (5), pp. 615–632, 2013.

COAD, A., FRANKISH, J., ROBERTS, R.G. and STOREY, D.J. *New Venture Survival and Growth: Does the Fog Llift? SPRU-Science and Technology Policy Research, Paper 202*, University of Sussex, 2012.

ROWLANDS, C. and GREAT BRITAIN, DEPARTMENT FOR BUSINESS, INNOVATION AND SKILLS *The Provision of Growth Capital to UK Small and Medium Sized Enterprises*, London, TSO, 2009.

Chapter 10

Current and future trends in finance for small and entrepreneurial businesses

The national market for small-business finance is made up from hundreds of thousands of funding choices and deals negotiated at a firm level, aggregated up to an overall picture. While the product-based analysis in previous chapters can be applied across a number of national markets, as in Chapter 3, a discussion of the national picture needs a sharper geographical focus as a case study.

The primary national focus of this chapter is the UK looking out from the great recession of 2007–2010 for the decade up to 2020. First, a short historical overview of developments in the last decade or so sets the scene. Second, the current market is reviewed using the UK SME Finance Monitor. Finally, comments on the likely pattern of market developments to 2020 concludes this review.

LESSONS FROM THE LAST DECADE

The long boom in UK economic growth led to well over a decade of continuous expansion of UK gross domestic product (GDP) and, perhaps, the most sustained period of profitability in the UK small-business sector since 1945. Business starts rose while closures lagged behind (and closures in financial distress fell sharply). Even allowing for a strong period of growth in property-based investment, capital spending by small firms on core plant and machinery grew as well and productivity increased.

Bank lending to small firms increased steadily in the years after 2000, although so did deposits and the sector as a whole remained in a fairly liquid position (i.e. net savings were evident with deposits exceeding borrowing). Overall profitability was strong enough to fund most of the required increase in working capital with overdraft facilities being used less regularly to fund a growing economy. This was probably assisted by the phased introduction of various forms of new late payment regulation (which had been seen as a big issue in the previous recessions). Credit card usage increased as well.

However, looking back now it is evident this buoyant general economic background disguised some worrying trends that became an issue when financial market turmoil in 2007 led to a subsequent deep and sustained real economy recession in 2008–2010.

- The upswing in capital spending, business creation and development depended too much on debt and too little on equity. Access to debt funding in a variety of forms became easier for all firms. Business owners diverted profits to savings or dividend payments and borrowed the money instead. Those seeking to set up a firm relied too much on borrowed funds, not personal resources.
- The growing involvement of non-high street banks in the SME lending market exacerbated the situation. Many were foreign-owned, often EU-based, strengthened by the launch of the Euro. Banks readily supplied new loans to entrepreneurs, often based on security drawn from rising property values. The non-high street banks were very active in this source of debt funding. Mortgage equity withdrawal and commercial mortgages provided a cheap form of funding for business ventures. The funds raised may have been used to inject equity to ventures but, too often, the source of funding was borrowed money rather than personal resources or wealth.
- In contrast, sources of equity funding for growing small firms had a more difficult decade, especially after the boom in high-tech stocks at the turn of the millennium. Many traditional suppliers moved away from supporting smaller equity deals and, with cheap borrowed money available in the UK, turned to other markets – especially in the Far East – to generate a good return for investors. Most of the equity-based initiatives from the early 1980s experienced problems, notably the over-the-counter (OTC) market and the alternative investment market (AIM). Business angel investment activity was hit hard by a number of attempts to reform the tax regime to minimise schemes to reduce revenue avoidance, as well as reforms to capital gains tax.
- Asset-backed lenders had a better period. However, invoice discounting fell out of favour with some professional advisers and, in some cases factoring especially was seen as evidence that the firm using this type of finance was in financial difficulties (especially as most firms had few cash-flow funding problems in a strong economy).

Put simply, when the real economy was hit hard in 2008–2010, over-reliance on borrowed money and a lack of an equity buffer commensurate with the expansion of earlier years led to more small firms having trouble meeting loan repayments. This was exacerbated by falling property values as well as some funding issues of a number of banks, leading to state intervention. The loss of business confidence, over capacity and falling profits reduced expansion plans, even amongst firms that were not over-geared. As a result, access to debt finance for small firms was at the centre of the debate about national economic recovery after 2007 (Figures 10.1–10.3).

However, even amongst the majority of established firms that were not over-geared and in financial difficulties after the boom period prior to 2007, it was a shock in subsequent years that the banks were no longer willing – and in some cases unable – to fund every project. In other cases, the funding was still available but the questions asked by the bank manager about development plans increased, also the terms and conditions on funding offers were tougher. Margins charged

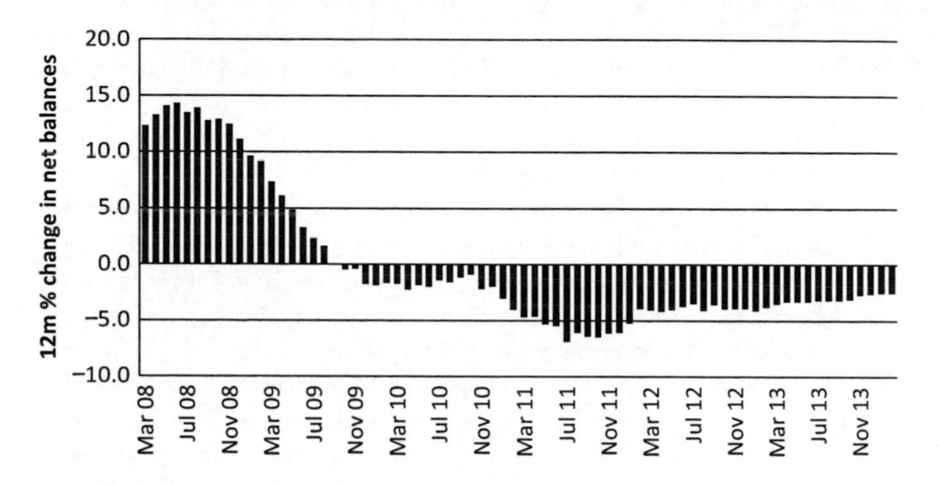

Figure 10.1
Net SME Lending Trends

Source: Bank of England, Trends in Lending, April 2014

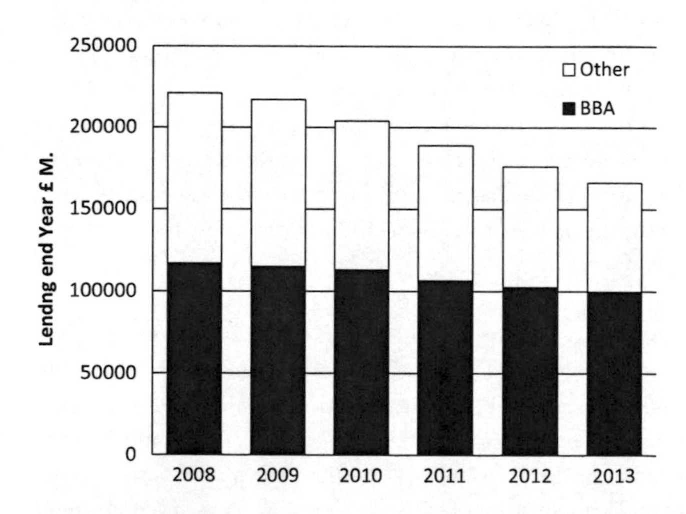

Figure 10.2
SME Lending by Bank Type

Source: RBS Independent Lending Review, BBA and BOE Statistics and author estimates

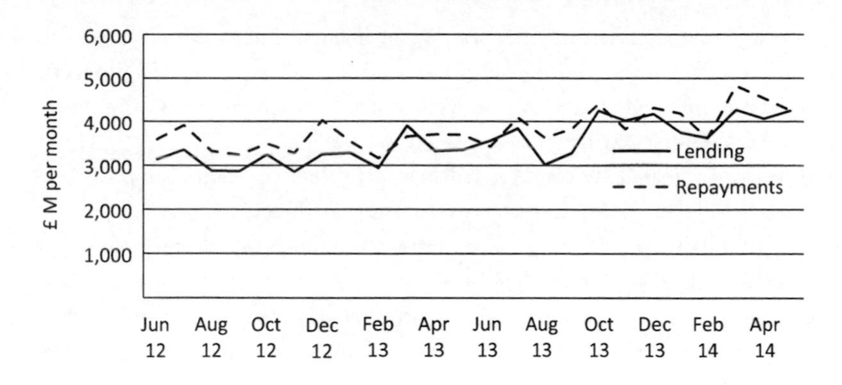

Figure 10.3
Gross Lending and Repayments

Source: BOE, Bankstats, May 2014

above the base rate went up as well (although most small firms did not pay more overall as the base rate fell to a record low level of 0.5%). It was a shock for many business owners who had survived the real economy recession that, when they did begin to think about new ventures again, the funding environment had changed so much (especially for debt finance).

A related but different issue emerged amongst start-ups and younger firms looking to set up a firm or borrow for expansion for the first time. Buoyant property values and the opportunity for mortgage equity withdrawal – or more generally easier access to personal credit – for most of the decade prior to 2007 allowed business founders to source the cash needed to start a business from funds borrowed elsewhere. When finance market conditions tightened in 2007–2008, in most cases, a new generation of start-ups had little previous experience of funding without access to cheap credit. This led to a revival of interest in bootstrap finance where firms try and fund pre-revenue activity using trade credit, leasing, factoring and credit cards as well as personal resources.

The combination of growing concerns about the terms of funding for established firms, combined with funding new and younger firms, reached a peak in mid-2008. The UK Government responded with the Enterprise Finance Guarantee scheme, the first of a long line of attempts to rebuild stability in the small-business finance market. The continuation of this 2008 measure and its successors – especially the Start-up Loan Scheme – in part shape the outlook for debt funding to 2020, as discussed below. In 2012, the Government announced the creation of the British Business Bank as a specialist funding agency to monitor and manage all the public interventions in the small-firm finance sector (debt and equity). The outlook to 2020 also takes account of the initial business plan of this new organisation announced in June 2013.

With the banking industry in turmoil and the cost of funds rising, equity markets still found it difficult to respond sufficiently to the challenges of small-firm funding leading to a shortfall in entrepreneurial finance. This was in contrast to funding for larger corporate businesses where equity and especially commercial bond markets stepped in as a viable source, notably when business confidence started to increase after 2010.

Ironically, more financially sound small firms still had substantial deposit balances but they preferred to sit on these reserves rather than invest. Consequently, the number of small firms seeking to use external finance fell sharply. Amongst those still actively looking for funding, greater attention was paid to leasing and invoice discounting as alternative traditional suppliers. However, all three areas of direct provision using crowdfunding to provide debt, equity and invoice finance had their UK origins in the years 2007–2010 as well.

THE SITUATION IN 2013

The UK SME Finance Monitor is the most representative and independent source of information on funding trends. Key trends are illustrated in Tables 10.1 and 10.2.

The key trends are:

- In the three years to 2013, about one-third of all SMEs used some form of external funding. This had fallen from over 50% in the three years to 2011.

Table 10.1 *The Use of External Sources of Finance by UK SMEs since 2002*

	Three Years Ending		*12m Ending Q4*	
Percentages	*2004*	*2007*	*2011*	*2013*
Use Any External Finance				
• *Now*			41	40
• *Last Three Years*	81	69		
• *Last Five Years*			44	43
Use of Different Types of Finance at Survey Date				
• *Bank Overdraft*	53	42	22	18
• *Term Loan or Mortgage*	24	19	8	9
• *Business Credit Card*	30+	28+	14	18
• *Asset Finance*	27	18	6	9
• *Asset-based Finance*	3	4	2	2
• *Grants*	6	5	1	1

	Three Years Ending		*12m Ending Q4*	
Percentages	*2004*	*2007*	*2011*	*2013*
• *Equity from family and friends*	<0.5	*	5	4
• *Equity from existing shareholders*	<1	*	4	4

Sources:
1) UKSMEFM, 2013Q4, pages 42, 44 and 46
2) S. Fraser, Finance for Small and Medium-Sized Enterprises: A Report on the 2004 UK Survey of SME Finance, Warwick Business School, 2005
3) A. Cosh, A. Hughes, A. Bullock, I. Milner, Financing UK Small and Medium-sized Enterprises: The 2007 Survey, Centre for Business Research, Cambridge, 2008

* Note that the questionnaire in 2007 was directly comparable
\+ Published as Personal or Business card but Business only data re-estimated by author to allow comparison

Table 10.2 *External Finance for SMEs in 2013 – Key Indicators*

		Employment			
Percent of firms in 2013	*All SMEs*	*0*	*1–9*	*10–49*	*50–250*
Using External Finance of any type	40	35	53	65	74
Injected Personal Funds into business	39	40	36	19	11
No plans to Seek External Finance	41	46	30	24	17

Source: SME Finance Monitor, Q42013 Report, tables pages 43, 51 and 62

- Much greater use was being made of personal funds and trade credit to provide additional financial resources to firms over this period, especially in the very smallest enterprises.
- Overall though, about 40% of firms were able to manage cash-flow and fund expansion from retained profits in the business. This suggests much of the excesses in terms of debt funding seen prior to 2007 especially had been reversed; indeed, this may have been over-corrected.
- Very few firms (under 5%) had approached any form of equity funding in the last three years, although where this had happened, the firms were fast growing with more significant growth ambitions.
- The predominant preference was for businesses not to seek external finance. Indeed, firms reported they were happy being in this situation. Where outstanding debts do exist, they were being paid off (this conclusion is supported by official Bank of England data that net borrowing by small firms fell in 2013).

THE FUTURE

As business confidence picks up, development plans will return and interest in external funding will increase yet again. As a consequence, it is reasonable to expect that demand for external funding to SMEs will rise over the next three to five years in a cyclical upswing. The exact timing is difficult to assess, as is the scale of the aggregate increase, both issues that concern policy makers and economic forecasters alike.

However, this is not the primary focus of interest in this study. Rather, given the upheaval in both the financial and real economy since 2007 has largely run its course, now is a very appropriate time to conclude this review of small-business and entrepreneurial finance by looking at how the trends in the market may evolve out to 2020. Will the pattern of activity seen prior to 2007 be re-established as many business owners seek, or will things be different? The simple answer is that, beyond a cyclical upswing in activity, many aspects of the UK SME finance market will change significantly over the next decade.

- The mainstream banking sector will continue to be cautious in the supply of entrepreneurial debt-based funding. Established, well-managed firms with a track record and a verifiable means of repayment will, like firms seeking straightforward cash-flow support, face few problems. Indeed, as business confidence recovers these types of firm will be commonplace allowing overall bank lending to rise. However, a growing number of special cases will face problems not seen in the years prior to 2007, especially start-ups and first-time borrowers with no track record. The caution of the banks, which will increasingly extend to the more recent entrants as well beyond the high street names, will largely be a product of regulatory reform and the higher underlying cost of funds. This could, in turn, encourage more formal market segmentation between traditional providers and alternative publicly backed funders such as the Community Development Finance Institutions (CDFIs) and the Start-up Loans Company.
- Amongst business owners and advisers, interest will continue to increase in alternative funding solutions. This will encompass traditional alternatives such as leasing and factoring, although much of this will come via new products and delivery channels (digital platforms and crowdfunding). The recent revival in worries about the competitiveness in the UK financial services sector will continue to grow, especially concerning the number of new entrants and the pace of expansion. The worries will mainly be about transparency in pricing and innovation rather than access to debt finance overall, in line with a growing economy. However, any subsequent competition inspired changes will take many years to shape the market.
- While overall access to debt finance worries should ease, as a consequence of remaining shortages of loan funding for some types of higher-risk activities,

demand for smaller-scale equity support for entrepreneurial funding will increase. Indeed, the emphasis of public debate on access to finance will move from debt funding to equity-related issues over the next few years. New innovations, such as the Business Growth Fund set up in 2010, have a key role in the years ahead to find solutions to the need for supporting equity investment, as do pension funds and long-term investors. This is also an issue that may require more attention from the tax authorities but this is currently being hampered by the tax avoidance debate.

- It is also possible that a more general shortage of debt funds for small firms may emerge. Regulatory change to the banking system such as ring-fencing may lead to banks preferring to use funding capacity to support personal lending products, especially when allied to changes in the international capital adequacy regulations. This may finally increase interest in wholesale securitisation of SME loan books to more significant levels than seen in the last decade.(Securitisation would allow banks to package up loans and on-sell to long-term investors, thus releasing capacity to lend to other small firms.)
- Much also depends on the role of public authorities, notably the new British Business Bank. The 15 or so years after the recession of the early 1990s until 2007 were driven by low regulation and free market solutions. Regulation and reform in the banking system is already moving to a much more active role for government in direct intervention in the SME finance market. Current plans for the British Business Bank to mainly centre on direct partnership investments to fill gaps identified in overall funding provision. How well this is executed in the equity market and the willingness of small-business owners to embrace equity funding where required is a key issue.
- We are also in a phase of innovation in the delivery of funding solutions to smaller firms. In the banking sector, technology is now available to speed up the credit decision and sanctioning process or even pre-approve loans. More of this will be done online or via the telephone, rather than face-to-face. Crowd-based funding and internet-based solutions to invoice discounting have already begun. The impact of regulatory change on some parts of this activity is uncertain, as will be the resilience to crowd-based lending when base rates rise. However, the technology is here to stay.

However, the fundamentals of small-business and entrepreneurial finance will remain the same.

Small firms seek external funding for two different reasons. Finance is sought for cash-flow funding to help a firm balance the books on a trading basis. Alternatively, external funding is needed to set up and later grow a business beyond its current trading format, referred to in this review as entrepreneurial funding.

Markets evolve, regulations change and the business cycle goes up and down. However, understanding the different reasons why a firm is looking for external funding is a timeless key to the world of small firm finance.

BIBLIOGRAPHY

BREEDON, T. and GREAT BRITAIN, DEPARTMENT FOR BUSINESS, INNOVATION AND SKILLS *Boosting Business Finance Options: Report of Industry-led Working Group on Alternative Debt Markets*, London, BIS (URN 12/668), 2012.

CENTRE FOR BUSINESS RESEARCH *UK Survey of SME Finances, 2007*, Published online, 2008: www.cbr.cam.ac.uk/research/projects/PEU13output.htm (accessed 10 July 2014).

FRASER, S. *Finance for Small and Medium-Sized Enterprises: Report on the 2004 UK Survey of SME Finances*, Published online, 2005: www.wbs.ac.uk/downloads/research/wbs-sme-main.pdf (accessed 10 July 2014).

FRASER, S. *Small Firms in the Credit Crisis: Evidence from the UK Survey of SME Finances*, Published online, 2009: www2.warwick.ac.uk/fac/soc/wbs/research/ei/latest/small_firms_in_the_credit_crisis_v3test.pdf (accessed 10 July 2014).

NESTA *The Rise of Future Finance: The Alternative Funding Benchmark Report 2013*, London, NESTA, 2014.

NIESR *Evaluating Changes in Bank Lending to SMEs over 2001–12 – Ongoing Tight Credit? NIESR Discussion paper No. 408*, Published online, 2013: www.niesr.ac.uk/sites/default/files/publications/dp408.pdf (accessed 10 July 2014).

Appendix I

Case studies in external finance for entrepreneurial and small firms

The case studies presented in this appendix illustrate examples of how a number of very different firms have approached business funding. The objective is to provide some more descriptive analysis to reinforce the main points developed in the book. In all cases, a descriptive narrative is followed by a discussion relating the actions described back to the main concepts of cash-flow and entrepreneurial funding outlined in Chapters 1 and 2. The case studies also support the longer-term 'roller-coaster' analysis developed in Chapter 9 (although a complementary review of MMC Ltd. is included in the chapter as well).

While all the case studies are based on actual businesses either mentored or researched by the author, to ensure confidentiality names and other details have been changed. However, no changes have been made to the key funding decisions or products used by the individual firms. Also, any financial data has been left unchanged.[1]

ISLAND ICE CREAM

Outline description

This is a small business run as a partnership with two sisters who live close to a farm owned by their parents. They make a luxury ice cream product in small quantities and sell it direct to local independent restaurants. All the customers are within about 25 miles of where the production takes place and pay for goods on delivery cash-in-hand. New customers are mainly found through personal recommendation.

The business started in an informal way, almost by accident. One of the sisters needed to raise some cash to boost income after the birth of her first child and the idea to make luxury ice cream seemed obvious as she made it as a hobby. The other sister came up with some of the more practical ideas. The parents' farm had a disused old dairy, and a small-scale ice cream pasteuriser, chiller and ageing vat combination unit was bought second hand via an internet auction site. The parents agreed to let the sisters use the dairy unit rent free for three years (although water and electricity were chargeable). They could also source milk and cream from the parents' herd and settle up for what they used at the end of the month.

The business started very easily. Most of the work now takes place on two days a week. One partner does most of the production on a Thursday. The other partner finishes off packaging and delivers on the Friday, ready for the weekend trade at the restaurants they supply. Nobody else works for the business. The two sisters do everything, fitting it around childcare and other family commitments. All the cash they receive is banked weekly. Invoiced bills are settled straight away, mainly using online banking. The only exception is the milk bill to the family farm that is paid at the end of the month.

Settlement of the monthly milk bill also provides a trigger for the sisters to work out what profit they have made and divide it up; they take three-quarters as drawings from the business in lieu of wages and the other quarter of net profit is left on deposit to save up. They realise that for a number of reasons this safety buffer is important. The equipment they have may need replacing at short notice. Also, at the end of the rent-free period they may need to fund upfront costs on a lease. A small delivery van may also need replacing in due course.

A full-year summary of income and outgoings in 2013/14 suggests that by selling 100 litres of wholesale ice cream a week they will have an annual turnover of about £18,200. At present, the net income after ingredients and other variable costs are paid for is about £7,250 a year (but they do not pay rent). The business was originally subsidised at the start with one sister loaning the partnership £500. The other sister borrowed £500 in a personal capacity to buy the second-hand van now used in the business (and now repaid). This loan was taken out just before she left full-time work to go on maternity leave so the bank looked at her salary as a source of repayment. The business now has £4,000 in a bank account and – based on the 25% set-aside rule – this should rise steadily now to over £6,200 over the next year. At the same time, the two partners take out about £70 a week each (effectively for one day's work).

Discussion

This appears to be a classic example of a hobby start-up, mainly out of necessity and using a fair degree of family support. However, these situations are very common in the small business environment. Even the smallest business still has to handle the basic needs of funding and cash management.

The partnership is currently trading profitably and needs no external funding to maintain its day-to-day operations. A personal capital injection and sourcing second-hand equipment got the business going. Cash-flow management is mainly achieved through the negotiation of favourable settlement terms from a major supplier (the farm). Also, the 25% set-aside rule ensures the buffer the business has to manage any income disruption is growing.

This business does not have any plans to expand, so it has no obvious need for entrepreneurial funding. However, even to fund a replacement for the plant and equipment could be a challenge over the next few years. A brand new production unit currently costs about £25,000 and they do not have enough free cash-flow to easily afford repayments (especially when the rent-free arrangement expires). The partners are thinking about taking the business to a more stable and long-term funding position through bringing in a silent partner to provide a cash injection. They have been in informal discussions with a restaurant owner they deal with to see if he is interested.

CHESIL BEACH CARS

Outline description

Chesil Beach Cars is a private car hire business that was set up in early 2011 in preparation for the Olympic Sailing events in Weymouth. The owner set up a firm to ferry VIPs and officials from a train station to a number of local hotels. He got a contract from three hotels for this work for the 12 months ending in October 2012. In total, the owner used about £10,000 of personal savings to set up the home-based business. Also, the hotel contract was enough to secure a bank loan to help buy a good second-hand vehicle and complete all the required registrations. The hotels pay an agreed rate per trip regardless of the number of people in the car. They pay via invoice normally 15 days after the end of month.

After the end of the Olympics, the business clearly had a difficult period of adjustment but the hotels remained loyal to Chesil Beach Cars based on price, reliability and good customer feedback. The owner took minimal income from the Olympic work – using personal savings and casual work as a source of income instead – and this built up as reserves that allowed the business to survive. He bought another second car for cash as well.

Over the last year or so, the business has continued to grow. Indeed, the business has changed as well to a new operating model. The owner now has three cars that he maintains and services as needed. He either drives one of the vehicles working for a small group of hotels, or rents them out to other drivers for a fee and they operate their own private hire operation. This way, all three vehicles are being driven for hire most times of the day and all week (unless maintenance is needed). The owner will also repair vehicles owned by other taxi firms, often at short notice for a premium fee.

The income mix of the business has changed as well. The owner still gets paid via invoice from a few hotels and this is reliable income. Also, he receives regular fixed cash payments from the drivers who rent his cars to operate a private hire business. When he works as a mechanic the owner also gets paid via an invoice as well. However, this repair work is less certain income than revenue from hotel work although very profitable when available. This mature and wide-ranging income mix has now allowed the owner to fund the third vehicle on a finance lease arrangement direct with the car manufacturer (who offer special schemes for high mileage vehicles used as a taxi).

As the business is changing and growing, it is difficult to get a true reading of underlying sales and profits in 2013/14. However, based now on three cars on the road, gross revenue is close to £100,000 a year with the only significant monthly repayments being on the new car lease of about £4,000 (as the bank loan to fund the first car has been repaid). Although other costs are high, especially insurance and fuel, two of his cars are also driven by other self-employed drivers. Overall, the owner has an annual profit of close to £30,000 a year at the moment. As a result, in the last six months he has started to take a regular income from the business for the first time (up till then, the owner for some time had a second job and took profits from the business in an ad hoc way). The owner has recently got married and the regular income will help his application for a residential mortgage.

Discussion

In contrast to the ice cream case study, this is an opportunity-based start-up where the owner has invested heavily at the beginning, secured a contract and a bank loan and worked for a long term without drawing profits. Now, this combined garage repair, car hire and taxi operation has few cash-flow-based issues as it has a long-standing arrangement with local hotels that pay on time and most of the other revenues are paid in cash. Rather, the business has needed to fund change and evolution over a couple of years through major investment. This has mainly come from the personal cash injection by the owner at the start and the continued reinvestment of profits from earlier contracts. He did also get a bank loan early on but has moved to a more appropriate lease-based funding source for the latest purchase.

The business may well have to go through a further evolution of funding at a later date. It may no longer be possible to operate this from a home base, especially if the lucrative car repair work is developed more. As long as the recent move to draw a regular salary does not get out of hand, the cash reserves should be sufficient to fund a lease payment for premises or maybe a commercial mortgage. An alternative could be to take in a business partner and bring some new equity on board.

EAGLE TOWERS PROPERTY DEVELOPMENT LTD.

Outline description

Eagle Towers was a development company set up specifically by property investors to purchase a run-down south coast hotel, demolish and then rebuild it into 20 retirement flats. The company had three founder investors and was run day-to-day by an experienced project manager working on a contract basis. The old hotel was bought with outline planning permission for redevelopment for £750,000 and the three investors raised £1 million overall from personal and family resources, allowing some working capital to cover the initial phases of the project (fees to the project manager, architects and legal costs) and the work on the initial group of five flats. The overall build was split into three phases with the exact timing of the final phase especially likely to be influenced by market conditions.

All the building work on phase one was subcontracted to a specialist contractor for a fixed price (including quality and delivery targets for the work). The projected selling price per unit (after legal costs) on the phase was £100,000 per unit. The land cost £37,500 per unit and on-site build costs were a further £30,000 a unit, leaving a projected profit from each flat of £32,500. Based on the projections from the first five units, across the whole three phases, the founder investors believed the redevelopment work should finally generate £650,000 profit from an initial £1 million investment.

Phase one built and sold according to plan. All five units sold within a month of them being marketed. Phase two for a further five units was started immediately using the same builder and a similar fixed price arrangement (building costs per unit went up slightly between phase one and two but this was more than offset by house price inflation, so profit margins in excess of 30% per unit continued).

However, early on in phase two, the project manager reported problems with build quality under the contract, as well as some slippage in the pace of construction. The investors became very worried that the early marketing for phase two would be wasted as potential buyers would go elsewhere. Indeed, the phase one site was adjacent to phase two. Completion of phase one also began to be impacted by work on-site with most of the new residents due to move into the new flats in the coming weeks (the overlap would increase further as phase two slipped behind schedule). As the five sales in phase one had been through exchange of contracts, if the completion did not occur on time, penalty clauses would be due.

As the worries of the investors mounted, the advice from the project manager was to bring the building work in-house. The building firm was in breach of both the quality and delivery targets in the phase two contract, and Eagle Towers had the right to end the contract without compensation (ensuring that the builder was paid for all the work actually completed and the materials on site). The project manager also knew that the building firm worked mainly through subcontractors anyway and Eagle Towers could work direct with them provided he was able to bring in a foreman as well.

As this revised project plan was implemented, the directors of Eagle Towers spotted a further problem. At the start of phase one, the investors provided £250,000 above the land purchase costs to start building work. After fees and legal costs, the project manager was left with £200,000 to pay for construction, enough to build between six or seven houses. The idea was that the proceeds from phase one would come on stream providing additional funds to complete phase two and so on, until all three phases were built. However, advance purchasing of materials by the builder, combined with the cost of hiring a foreman and worries about delays to the legal completions from phase one, had the potential to quickly lead to a cash-flow problem.

The solution for the directors of Eagle Towers was to accelerate the start of phase three. Although this strategy required additional working capital it was obtained by a deal struck with a national chain of care homes for elderly people who were looking to diversify into development activity. The care home owner invested £400,000 into Eagle Towers for just under 30% equity share of the business. This investment was sufficient to overcome any worries over the cash-flow for phase two, as well as provide resources for phase three.

Eagle Towers Property Development Ltd. only traded for three years and was wound up before its fourth anniversary. All 20 properties were sold and house price inflation ensured that the phase three units averaged £115,000 each. As a result, the total project revenue was £2.150 million against land and building costs of £1.430 million. Consequently, the original three investors received a combined gross development profit of £511,000 and the care home chain £209,000.

Discussion

Construction and real estate-related businesses account for nearly one in five SMEs so the example of Eagle Towers is not uncommon. Speculative real estate development presents a number of challenges for firms seeking debt funding (unlike builders who are working on a contract basis). This is because such projects only generate funds to repay debt on completion and, until then, the work consumes cash well in advance of any security value. (In contrast, a contract builder would work to a schedule and normally receive stage payments to cover any loan repayments.)

Taking this consideration into account, the £1 million founder equity set up the venture on a solid base. The initial plan was to use the equity invested as initial stake to support the lifetime of the project, combined with some careful cash-flow management in the scheduling of sales receipts from the various phases of activity. This plan was reinforced by the fixed price costs negotiated for phase one and part of phase two.

Unlike most of the case studies discussed in this chapter, the business no longer exists and was wound down after the building work was completed. The project was a success, although the funding plan had to be modified and a new third-party investor brought in to ensure success (although this decision reduced the returns to the original investors, albeit this impact was offset by market price inflation on the selling values on phase three units). Even when facing a cash-flow problem, the original investors decided to raise more equity rather than seek an overdraft. Moreover, when the building work was taken over by Eagle Towers, no other finance products were used by the business as the construction activity was still undertaken by subcontractors.

A final observation is that the funding decisions made by the owners of Eagle Towers and the external finance sources used illustrate that the distinction between cash-flow and entrepreneurial activity can become blurred. As discussed in Chapter 1, speculative real estate is an activity in which this often happens. As this is a one-off project, the cash-flow and entrepreneurial aspects of funding have merged into one. Only by raising enough funds to underpin cash-flow can the entrepreneurial objective of the business be achieved. This provides a contrast with, for example, a manufacturing activity where funds raised to underpin research and development activity provides an entrepreneurial boost to the order book, followed by a production phase where cash-flow needs to be sustained to fund output to fulfil contracts.

DAVE-ANNE STORES LTD.

Outline description

Dave-Anne Stores Ltd. (DAS) is a business owned by a husband and wife team and they now operate two retail shops selling a wide range of groceries and associated goods to the local community. The business was started a few years ago with one shop. The couple used the proceeds of a family inheritance and their own savings to purchase a lease on a suitable vacant shop and to refit the premises.

DAS is a success, although it is a low-margin operation and requires long hours of work. A second shop located in another part of the same town was added two years after start-up using the same funding method to acquire the lease. Both shops now generate revenue of about £100,000 each a year. Each shop had a surplus over all costs of about £10,000 in the last year after the directors had drawn a salary and these funds are currently being retained in the firm. The business hopes to add further units in future years.

Apart from the directors, all the staff are part time. Over 90% of sales receipts are in the form of cash or debit card transactions over the counter (the directors do allow a couple of firms close to the shops to have a monthly account for purchases settled by invoice and internet banking soon after the end of each month).

DAS is part of a wholesale buying chain that will supply all deliveries during a month on account. The invoice needs to be paid within the first five days of the next calendar month. However DAS collects revenue on a daily basis to meet this bill (as well as a regular VAT bill). As a result, beyond deposit and current accounts, the only external finance products used by DAS are leasing facilities for the small van acquired to move stock between the two premises and for certain items of equipment in the shops (the tills and display freezers). The use of leasing made sense as profits are modest, regular payments also matched income streams and in both cases the goods came with a maintenance contract from the supplier.

Discussion

DAS is very typical of many smaller retail firms. The core initial funding came from a family inheritance not debt and the two directors wanted to set up a business that in effect also provides them with a job. The use of a wholesale buying arrangement has effectively provided a solution to any cash-flow management needs of the business, especially as they are mainly paid in cash. DAS is a regular user of the local high street bank as it needs to pay in cash on a daily basis but they have no current debt or any immediate plans to start borrowing. Some of the key shop equipment is leased with a maintenance agreement.

Although DAS does not have any immediate plans to expand further, this remains the medium-term aim. A consideration could be the method of funding any further expansion. On the two previous occasions, DAS have used a family inheritance to pay the premium of a new shop lease plus fitting out costs. The property is then rented on a monthly basis. This way the premises could be occupied with minimal capital outlay. However, for a third property they would probably have another option as well.

DAS now has a track record is setting up and running profitable retail stores. This will be recognised by a bank if they sought a commercial mortgage to purchase the freehold on a third outlet. The monthly accounting surplus from the initial two outlets held in the accounts would fund a deposit and pay for legal costs, while future revenue surplus would cover mortgage payments (indeed, this may not be needed as DAS would not need to pay rent on the new property anyway).

Regardless of the method used to fund the acquisition of a new outlet, most of DASs other finance arrangements will easily extend to a third site, notably the wholesaling account and equipment leasing. It would appear that the main issue about expansion may not be one of raising the finance. Rather, a new outlet would have other implications for DAS. At present, each partner can look after one outlet providing oversight and control. A new outlet would require them to appoint a manager for one of the units as well (they have no suitable extended family members to ask to fill this role).

BLUE BIRD RECRUITMENT AGENCY LTD.

Outline description

Blue Bird is an online recruitment agency. It has five employees who work a mixture of part and full-time hours. All are home-based. The website was set up and is maintained by the business owner who also works as a recruitment agent. The business has no premises. Rather, the owner provides each agent with a laptop, a mobile phone and pays for a broadband line. The owner runs the firm now as a limited company. It was originally unincorporated but this proved difficult to sustain given the need to hold liability insurance (and it also helped with the funding arrangements).

The business started a few years ago with minimal funding needs, all drawn from the personal savings of the founder. At start-up, the owner limited the services offered to undertaking background checks and arranging interviews for candidates looking for work at a large local employer. This was a contract arrangement to help the firm's in-house human resources (HR) team. From this and a couple of follow-on projects, enough contacts were made to develop a recruitment business. A website came along a bit later and members of staff were added one at a time as the business grew. On each phase of expansion the funding needs were still minimal (a mobile phone, laptop and broadband line).

As with a wide range of service-based operations, the recruitment business is a people-based activity. The business relies heavily on the network of contacts between staff and those responsible for recruitment at a large number of businesses both at a regional and national level. The operation also now depends on the website as this provides a way for candidates to upload their CVs, sift through vacancies and monitor the progress of applications.

Until recently, the day-to day finance needs of the business were also fairly straightforward. Firms looking for staff pay fees for the work done. A proportion of the fee – somewhere between a third and a half – is paid when Blue Bird is engaged to find a recruit. The balance due is paid after the new member of staff starts work. The final payment is often paid in arrears.

When the business was young this pattern of split fee income used to be sufficient to meet cash-flow needs – mainly the monthly bills for staff wages and commission – but, as the business grew month-on-month, the owner often had a funding problem. As a result, Blue Bird set up an account with an invoice discounting provider. This arrangement allows Blue Bird to draw funds against the unpaid portion of the fee after recruitment has been agreed. Without such an arrangement, the firm often had to wait for 30 or 60 days after a person had started work before the funds were received. The discounter has looked at Blue Bird's client base and selected 20 blue-chip and national names they deal with on a regular basis. Blue Bird can draw up to 85% of the value of the unpaid invoices owed by these 20 firms from the discounter at any point of time. This is normally enough to manage any cash-flow issues, especially at the time of the monthly wage bill. This has proved a cost-effective way of eliminating funding worries. The monthly fee has to be paid regardless of use but the interest charge on a daily basis for the funds advanced is often quite low.

A problem over the last 12 months is that two blue-chip customers have insisted that the initial engagement fee should be removed and they will settle the full sum when a candidate is engaged. In return, they have agreed to pay the amount due on the same day that the new recruit actually starts work, rather than in arrears. This development has the potential to undermine the current funding plan (especially if more companies take this approach). The loss of the initial engagement fee will reduce cash-flow even though members of staff are taking on more work. Earlier payment in full is welcome but the owner is worried that the firm providing the invoice discount service may conclude that the pool of debt owed by blue-chip firms is being reduced and seek to renegotiate the full arrangement.

Blue Bird's owner does have a back-up plan. A discussion with the bank where the business has a current account suggests a straightforward overdraft facility could be agreed. The bank is able to see an established pattern of credits into the account as well as the monthly outgoings for wages and commission. The current use of the second stage payments from blue-chip firms as security for the invoice discount facility will limit the size of any overdraft facility agreed. This is because the bank will acknowledge the discounter would have preferential rights to these funds. However, a small facility will be sufficient for Blue Bird to be confident about its day-to-day funding going forward.

Discussion

Blue Bird has grown from very small beginnings to a sizeable business, albeit still wholly online and without premises. Growth has been incremental but, as the firm specialises in filling senior roles, fee income is about £36,000 a month (equivalent to each adviser placing 10 roles a month for a £600 fee). Consequently, annual turnover is now in excess of £430,000 a year. The owner pays his staff about £250,000 a year in salary and commission with website and IT increasing costs by a further £50,000. As a result, the owner has a surplus for about £130,000 a year that can be used for salary, dividends or saved as retained earnings.

The funding arrangements for Blue Bird are also well thought out. Its funding needs are solely cash-flow related. Recruitment firms often use asset financing, more typically a confidential invoice discounting arrangement as in the case of this firm. It is a little surprising that the arrangement has been in place for a while. Most invoice discounting facilities have a minimum turnover size and even with sales at the current level the business would be too small for some suppliers.

A move to an overdraft facility also appears a sensible option, either as a back-up facility or as a full cash-flow funding arrangement. It may be better for the owner to unwind the discounting facility especially if more blue-chip firms move to a single payment option as the interest rate on the associated debt facility could rise.

However, a financial adviser looking at the overall results of the business may also express some medium-term concerns. The owner is drawing nearly all the profits out of the business and did not create a fund of core capital at start-up to see the business through any cash-flow issues. As a result, the business has always been close to a cash-flow problem when salary and commissions are paid. Another strategy would be to either put some of the funds withdrawn back into the firm as a capital injection, or at least allow some earnings to be retained going forward. This way a capital buffer may well reduce or even eliminate the cash-flow worries in the future.

FINN-BARR DATA BUILD

Outline description

This business was formed by two graduates who met at university in 2002, one a computer scientist (Finn) and the other an accountant (Barr). Since leaving university they have both had successful independent careers but stayed in touch on a social basis. However, in early 2013 the IT specialist came up with an idea to collect and combine real-time market information on a niche business segment to support financial decision making by banks and investors. The concept uses most of the 'big data' tools increasingly commonplace in data and management information circles.

However, Finn quickly realised he did not have much financial expertise and only limited savings to fund the development of the idea and approached Barr to see if he could help. The outcome of a discussion over a number of meetings was agreement to work together to set up a business to take the idea forward. A limited company was set up and by the start of 2014 the two directors had each used £5,000 of personal savings to fund some preliminary legal work and secure adequate intellectual property rights on the concept. Finn and Barr were still in full-time work with long-term employers; both are married with existing family and mortgage commitments.

Both directors realised the business was still in a fledgling position with significant work to do. Funding was needed to test and build the data systems and market the product to a number of larger commercial clients. The business would probably take three or four years to develop in full, but in the next 12 months they needed £100,000 funding to take ideas forward and then hoped to generate initial orders followed by rising revenue streams in subsequent years. In January 2014, the projection was that first orders were unlikely before summer 2015 at the earliest. Looking further ahead, after four or five years, initial thinking was that the business should be sold. Although estimates of market growth and income were very tenuous, taking a medium-term view, if the business could eventually provide advice on one-in-ten deals in its market niche and get paid 1% of the associated revenue, this would be £3 million a year in full-year fee income with projected margins of over 50%.

Neither of the two directors – nor immediate family members – had any significant cash savings to fund this longer-term development activity. In particular, neither director had any housing equity and both are too young to draw on pension savings funds. Indeed, the next phase of work would require at least one of them to give up employment to concentrate on the project full time. They looked at the opportunity for any grant aid but this appeared unlikely to be successful. The only way forward was to seek some form of equity investment as, in the short term at least, traditional debt funding was not an option.

The size of the equity injection needed to fund the next stage of business development was well within the scope of a single business angel or a professional investment syndicate. However, both owners were worried about approaching this type of investor. This is because the size of the investment needed would be very significant compared with the stake the two founders held. They could not put in additional personal funds to avoid any equity dilution. Rather, they devised a strategy to persuade a larger group of investors to invest smaller amounts. The prospectus prepared suggested the business in a few years' time will be worth £1.5 million and they sought people to collectively invest £100,000 for 25% of the company. If achieved, this would represent a 375% return over a three or four-year period. The funding plan acknowledged the project is still untested and carries a number of risks but the founders believe the potential for return to be very attractive to offset the risk.

In order to avoid approaching business angels, Finn and Barr finally decided to use a crowdfunding equity platform to find investors. The project was listed on line for 12 weeks and secured 25 investors (typically investing £5,000 to £10,000 each with a range between £1,000 and £15,000). The money has been raised. Finn now works full time on the project and the directors hope to start test marketing in a few months' time. However, no orders have been won yet and dividends to shareholders are still some way off.

Discussion

It will be several months at least before the likelihood of success for this venture is more evident. However, the funding strategy adopted by Finn and Barr was bold. Quite correctly, the prospects for any commercial debt funding were judged to be non-existent. The business at the time of the fund raising did not have a marketable product, let alone any orders. As a result, any external funding had to be based around equity. Rather, Finn and Barr were very strongly opposed to approaching traditional angel investors. The reasons for this were partly financial – notably the fear of dilution and control – but also linked back to the style of business they sought to develop. Finn especially was keen to involve data experts in his investor group and hoped the use of the crowdfunding equity route would offer a chance for very small investors to get involved. This appears to have been a success based on the size of the investments. Also, several alumni from Finn and Barr's university year have reportedly made an investment.

Many owners in the position of Finn and Barr would have welcomed the chance to work with experienced equity investors, especially if this brought management support and advice as well. The deliberate attempt to avoid this route was a bold step that in terms of fund raising has been a success. The other alternative source of funding, such as a loan or shareholding investment with an existing data services supplier or financial services business, does not appear to have been considered at all.

DAPPER TEXTILES LTD.

Outline description

Dapper Textiles is a business created through a management buy-in. The business was originally a subsidiary of a larger firm and it was sold off to raise funds for a new venture about 10 years ago. Three entrepreneurs, an accountant and two experienced textile business owners, were approached by the original owner to see if they were interested in the deal. At the time, the business had a turnover of about £1 million per year with pre-tax profits of £100,000 and a workforce of 10 long-term employees. The firm specialised in high-quality, low-volume, customised curtain production. In many cases, these were one-off designs for the heritage/conservation market. The business was offered for sale at £500,000. The price – equal to five times current profits – appeared high but it did include the freehold of the old traditional production site in the north of England plus the business had a reasonable and stable forward order book.

The prospective management team were interested but could not raise the £500,000 asking price. Indeed, the three investors could only collectively manage £60,000. As a result, funding for the deal was sourced from the private equity market. The funding was secured from a private equity fund that targeted buy-in or buy-out deals. They acquired 88% of the equity (and the right to appoint two non-executive directors) based on a five-year business plan for diversification and business growth which included:

- The development of an off-the-shelf range of products to build on the firm's heritage reputation. This would include curtain manufacture as well as associated household furnishings.
- A doubling in the firm's export sales.
- Improved production quality and flexibility achieved through investment in new production and design capabilities.
- Diversification into direct sales via a mail order operation and a factory shop on site.
- At least a five-fold rise in pre-tax profits after five years. The transformational change in the plan should have created a business with a value in excess of £2.5 million by year five, when the management team envisaged an exit from the investment would be achieved through on-sale.
- The funding agreement also included strict objectives around management costs and fees. Although two of the three directors had a track record in delivering a plan of this scale before, all three of the buy-in team would have a large part of remuneration linked to growth and business performance and eventual sale.

Ten years on and Dapper Textiles continues to trade. The buy-in appears to have done a very good job in delivering the original plan and going beyond that phase into one of further growth. However, the original private equity deal proved to be only the start of a number of phases of external finance raising and activity to achieve the goal.

In year one, the main emphasis was on revamping the existing production line with new tooling and equipment to allow both production quality to be increased and to prepare the factory for diversification of the product range. The firm was acquired debt-free with a freehold on the site and a largely unutilised overdraft facility. However, new equipment was almost exclusively acquired through a finance lease. Technology was evolving rapidly at the time with the introduction of computer-controlled weaving and cutting facilities. This increased the attractiveness of renting equipment with a maintenance deal rather than purchase and ownership. The business also had a steady order book to fund lease repayments.

Also in year one greater attention was paid to the export market with the appointment of three overseas sales executives. This activity needed funding and the cost of overseas travel proved more expensive than budgeted. The three directors met this unexpected cost by investing the proceeds of their annual performance bonus as a cash injection to purchase new equity (the equity fund managers agreed to this and a modest dilution in the majority shareholding of the fund from 88% to 80%).

In years two and three, Dapper concentrated mainly on new products and developing a direct retail activity. Orders had begun to rise based on work done in year one. The firm had to begin using its long-standing overdraft facility for cash-flow purposes. However, overall profits increased as well. With the agreement of the equity fund, the profits were used within the business rather than paid out as dividends to fund a new in-house design team and household furnishing products to sell alongside curtains.

However, additional funding was needed during year three to develop a retail outlet on vacant land at the production plant and to invest in a new website and retail order facility (the plan to develop a mail order business was dropped). This was funded in part through a commercial mortgage on the production site (with repayments linked to the rising order book). However, this was not enough to fund the next expansion phase. The equity fund agreed to a second round of funding provided all three of the original directors took part as well so shareholdings were not altered. A second round of £100,000 equity was raised this way in year three to complete the work.

The final part of the original five-year plan saw the business grow and build upon the changes made in years one to three. Profits increased to close to £700,000 by the end of year five, exceeding the plan. Total staff employed rose to 60. The higher level of profitability came mainly from the new products and the direct retail sales, both of which were higher margin activities than first planned. Export sales concentrated on more traditional products.

At the end of year five, the private equity fund reviewed its investment. The company was valued at £3.5 million (net of debts – the commercial mortgage of £75,000). The book value of the fund's total investment was £580,000 but no dividends had been paid in the five years. The equity partners now had a shareholding valued at £2.8 million (the three founder directors had shares valued at £700,000). For both the equity fund and the buy-in team, these results represented a substantial return on the original investments (in excess of 400%).

In the subsequent five years, Dapper has continued to grow, although sales did plateau in 2010–2012 before growing again in 2013. It now has nearly 100 staff and an annual turnover of £7 million. The original equity partner did not sell on the investment in full. Rather, it was agreed to sell half its stake (40%) to a follow-on equity fund for £1.5 million with one of the non-executive director roles being transferred as well. The business has continued to invest, mainly using finance leasing for its production facilities, although the commercial mortgage is being paid off as well. However, spurred on by the needs of the new equity partners, the target is to seek to pay a dividend each year now, subject to market conditions. As a result, Dapper has funded the most recent expansion to its retail activities using debt rather than equity (assisted by a tie-in with a national retail chain and a heritage charity with over three million members).

Discussion

The example of Dapper Textiles illustrates how the correct approach to business acquisition and planning requires both entrepreneurial people and funding. In this case, apart from a very small amount of personal investment by three people, the key to unlocking the potential for growth was achieved by linking these entrepreneurial people with a suitable equity investor. While the private equity industry has at times received a degree of criticism from commentators about its scale of commitment to the SME sector, in reality the example of Dapper Textiles shows how this source of funding can help three entrepreneurs execute a well thought out business plan. The scale of change in the business has been very significant and the number of firms that achieve the growth on a scale like Dapper is very small but they do exist.

This case study also illustrates additional issues such as:

- The interaction between private equity and other forms of funding, notably the overdraft, commercial mortgage and leasing, to fund different aspects and phases and growth.
- The linkages between different parts of the private equity market. The initial investment was undertaken by a specialist fund concentrating on management buy-in transactions. Half this stake was then sold after five years to a fund looking for more mature medium-term investments.

Of course, the funding needs of Dapper Textiles continue to evolve. The next phase may well have to address the future plans of the three original investors. They have now all made a significant gain on their original investments. Also, the 40% ownership stake from the first equity fund is likely to come up for review and they may be looking to withdraw totally.

COMPARING CASE STUDIES

These case studies have been selected to illustrate a number of different issues on the way that firms handle cash-flow and entrepreneurial funding. In different ways, all the examples are essentially successful and profitable operations, albeit on different scales.

Looking at a summary of the sources of external funding, it is important to remember that the studies cover a wide range of businesses over different phases of development and economic conditions. In some cases, they look at events in a business over a few months, in others many years. However, a few points drawn from the summary analysis in this appendix can be found in Table AI.1 that support the analysis in the main chapters.

Table AI.1 *Case Study Summary of Sources of External Finance used*

Case Study name	*External Funding used*						
	TD	*CM*	*OD/CC*	*F*	*L*	*FE*	*EE*
Island Ice Creams	*					*	
Chesil Beach Cars	*				*	*	
Eagle Tower Property						*	*
Dave-Anne Stores					*	*	
Blue Bird Recruitment			*	*		*	
Finn-Barr Data						*	*
Dapper Textiles		*	*		*	*	*
Midland Motor +		*			*	*	*

Key
TD = Term Debt
CM = Commercial Mortgage
OD/CC = Overdraft or Credit Card
F = Factoring or Inv. Discounting
L = Leasing
FE = Founder Equity
EE = External Equity

+Note Midland Motor is the case study included in Chapter 9

1. The role of founder equity is often forgotten in looking at funding as it provides the foundation on which external suppliers and investors are likely to support a business.
2. Beyond the common thread of founder equity, the range of external funding sources used is wide ranging. It would be very difficult to look at a typical SME.
3. External funding needs evolve over time. None of the case studies had a fixed pattern of external funding throughout the time periods under review.
4. Too much concentration on debt funding can easily lead to an unrepresentative view of the SME funding market. Only a minority of firms, for example, use any form of structured term debt.

Appendix II

International data

The review of the UK and comparable international data in Chapter 3 highlighted the importance of recognising the role of the national business environment in the choice of external financial products. Additional comments about business conditions were discussed in Chapter 9. As a result, most of the analysis in this study has drawn on UK data and experience. However, other data sources are available to look at the wider international context.

EUROPEAN UNION SURVEYS

Within the EU – especially the EU-29 grouping – greater efforts have been made in recent years to collect more data on SME finance on a standardised basis. As a result, a clearer picture is beginning to emerge. The latest EU-29 results are summarised in this appendix in Table AII.1, although it is still necessary to group together some product areas to provide robust results.

In terms of the products used, averaged across the EU-29 membership, the range looks very similar to the UK data reviewed in Chapter 3 (Table 3.1). UK SMEs report slightly higher use overall of debt-linked external sources of funding than in the EU-29. However, the mix of debt products is different. In the EU-29 as a whole, the core cash-flow management products – the bank overdraft and credit card – are used with lower frequency than in the UK. In contrast, greater use is made of term debt and asset-backed lending.

However, despite the best attempts of the EU statisticians to adjust for national differences, it is still likely that country results can be heavily influenced by local market definitions and tax considerations. As discussed in Chapter 3, these apparent variations in external funding need to be interpreted with care; they may be just as much to do with the structure and ownership of the financial institutions and the role of state-backed development banks in different countries as any variation in SME owner preference for different types of product. A similar comment is equally valid when looking at the results suggesting firms in the UK use slightly more equity than business based elsewhere in the EU-29.

As a result, looking at a summary of the data in Table AII.2 on the basis of three categories of funding provides better clarity. These categories are internal funds, debt and equity sources.

Such an analysis confirms that across some of the major national economies within the EU, aggregate use of external finance products shows a high degree of correlation, notably between the UK and Germany. (France is similar as well, although internal funds and retained profits were curtained in 2013/14, probably an indication of economic conditions in recent years). Within the EU-29 group

Table AII.1 *Sources of External Finance for SMEs in the EU-29 Member States, 2013*

External Finance used in last six months (to October 2013)	*Percent of all SMEs*
Bank – overdraft, credit line or credit card	39
Leasing, hire purchase, factoring	35
Bank loan	32
Other loan (including from family and friends)	15
Equity – shares	5
Equity – securities, subordinated debt etc	2
For reference:	
Internal funds	26
Trade credit	32
Grant or subsidised loan	13

Source: Eurostat, 2013 SMEs' Access to Finance Survey, 2013

Table AII.2 *Summary of SME Funding Sources in the EU-29 Member States, 2013*

Percent of all SMEs Using Source in 2013	*EU-average*	*EU-low**	*EU-high**	*UK*	*Germany*	*France*
Internal Funds	26	7	40	30	37	22
Debt	75	52	85	85	78	78
Equity shares	5	<1	45	9	6	8

Source: Eurostat, 2013 SMEs' Access to Finance Survey, 2013

*The range of results within the EU-29 grouping. Country varies by measure. High = Austria (internal funds), Ireland and UK (debt) and Latvia (Equity). Low = Portugal (internal funds), Latvia (debt) and Portugal (equity).

Note values can exceed 100 as multiple sources are reported.

some very wide variations are evident but it appears that these are mainly from the post-1995 accession states. Greater comparability is reported amongst the core pre-1990 EU membership which, in turn, represents the more developed national economies. Even so, the UK shares with Ireland the highest level of use of debt (at 85%), above the EU-29 average (75%).

WORLD BANK AND OECD SURVEYS

Chapter 3 included a discussion of the results from a major World Bank survey in the decade to 2000 on the pattern of SME external financing from a wide range of international markets inside and outside the EU. More up-to-date analysis has not been undertaken so far (the current series of World Bank Enterprise Surveys concentrate on emerging economies). However, ongoing work by the OECD into the business environment does include an SME scoreboard survey. This provides the only regular reliable source of data and even then this can only be used to look at very broad trends in the pattern of external SME financing, as summarised in Table AII.3, which compares the size of the market for venture capital and SME bank debt in a range of countries scaled to the national SME population. The results are presented in a format referenced to the UK market (where the UK = 100).

As discussed already, international results of this type are influenced heavily by different national market conditions as well as the composition of the economy and the business stock. Nevertheless, it is interesting to observe that the relative dependence of the UK SME sector on debt rather than equity – noted in the

Table AII.3 *International Comparisons – Size of National Markets compared with the UK*

Ratio UK = 100	*Venture Capital*	*SME Bank Loans*
UK	100	100
EU-8	26	90
USA	102	39
Canada	67	68
New Zealand	3	58
Russian Federation	238	20
Korea	13	85

Source: Author's calculations based on data in OECD, Financing SMEs and Entrepreneurs, 2014: An OECD Scoreboard, accessed online www.oecd.org/cfe/smes/financing-smes-scoreboard-2014.htm (accessed 27th August 2014).

Note that the data mainly relates to 2012. The definitions used are those provided in the OECD survey dataset and may differ from other sources. Underlying data converted from national currency to Euros based on end July 2014 exchange rates.

EU-29 results – is still evident in this more basic wider international analysis. This even appears to be the case when the UK is compared with the USA; in the latter, the venture capital market on a scaled-adjusted basis is slightly larger than the UK but the stock of SME debt is much lower.

OTHER NATIONAL SURVEYS

Very few national surveys are undertaken to match the regularity and detail in the UK SME Finance Monitor that has been used for much of the core data in this analysis. References have been included below for noteworthy examples in the USA, Canada and New Zealand.

DATA SOURCES

World Bank and OECD

World Bank Business Environment Survey: www.go.worldbank.org/RV060VBJU0 (accessed 8 September 2014).

World Bank Enterprise Surveys: www.enterprisesurveys.org/Data (accessed 8 September 2014).

OECD SME Benchmark Data: www.oecd.org/cfe/smes/ (accessed 8 September 2014).

European Union

EU SME Access to Finance Survey baseline report: www.ec.europa.eu/enterprise/policies/finance/files/2013-safe-analytical-report_en.pdf (accessed 8 September 2014).

European Central Bank Access to Finance Survey: www.ecb.europa.eu/stats/money/surveys/sme/html/index.en.html (accessed 8 September 2014).

National surveys

USA

US Federal Reserve Board Small Business Finance Survey (to 2003): www.federalreserve.gov/pubs/oss/oss3/nssbftoc.htm (accessed 8 September 2014).

The US Federal Reserve has not updated the 2003 so far but the work is undertaken at state level. A good example is the New York Reserve Bank SME Credit Survey: www.newyorkfed.org/smallbusiness/ (accessed 8 September 2014).

Many other surveys are available in the USA, normally by the State Reserve Bank but some tend to concentrate on bank-related credit conditions. For example, see the Federal Reserve of Atlanta dataset: www.frbatlanta.org/research/smallbusiness/sbsurvey/ (accessed 8 September 2014).

Canada

SME Research and Statistics – Financing: www.ic.gc.ca/eic/site/061.nsf/eng/h_02683.html (accessed 8 September 2014).

SME Finance benchmarking tool: www.ic.gc.ca/eic/site/pp-pp.nsf/eng/home (accessed 8 September 2014.)

New Zealand

Business Finance Survey 2004: www.stats.govt.nz/browse_for_stats/businesses/business_finance.aspx (accessed 8 September 2014).

Index